D0498766

BLOND CHI

A Shanghai Interlu

Hannnelore Heinemann Headley

A young Hannelore at the Berlin Zoo, May 7, 1938

安娜樂麗

Blond China Doll Enterprises
Triple H Publishing

© All rights reserved. This book is protected by copyright. No part of this book may be reproduced in any form or by any means, including photocopying, or utilized by any information storage and retrieval system without written permission from the copyright owners.

Blond China Doll Enterprises
Triple H Publishing
71 Queen Street
St. Catharines, ON
L2R 5G9
www.blondchinadoll.com

Library and Archives Canada Cataloguing in Publication

Headley, Hannelore Heinemann, 1936-
Blond China Doll : A Shanghai Interlude,
1939-1953 / Hannelore Heinemann Headley.

ISBN 0-9735803-0-5

1. Headley, Hannelore Heinemann, 1936-. 2. Jews, German-China-Shanghai-Biography. 3. Refugees, Jewish-China-Shanghai-Biography. 4. Shanghai (China)-Biography. I. Title.

DS135.C5H42 2004 951'.132004'9240092 C2004-903735-8

First edition

Cover map used with permission by SinoMedia Shanghai, www.talesofoldchina.com
Shoah letter used with permission by the Shoah Foundation
Back cover photo used with permission by The St. Catharines Standard.
Photo by Bob Tymczyszyn

Book design and layout by Craig A. Bondy of Byond Communication
Prepared for publication by Solotext Editorial

Disclaimer: The historical references within this book have been cross-referenced from public record. This book is not intended for academic use. The statements made and opinions expressed are the personal observations and assessments of the author based on her own experience and were not intended to prejudice any party. Every effort has been made to make this book as complete and as accurate as possible. However, there may be errors, both typographical and in content. It is the preference of Triple H Publishing to use "Blond" as a non-gendered term.

~ To the memory of my dear parents,
Paula and Heinz Heinemann, whose courage
made this story possible

In remembrance of
the countless who could not escape ~

ha•no•lo•li
(Chinese translation of Hannelore)

Preface

In the past decade or so, the Jewish experience in Shanghai has slowly made its rightful way from what was once a footnote to a more prominent place in the pages of history. Through books and documentaries, mostly by survivors or their children, more and more people are becoming aware of the role Shanghai played during the Holocaust. The lives of my family and that of many others were saved by the fortunate opportunity of finding refuge in this haven. With this book, I am not attempting to further document what historians and some of the survivors who were adults during their stay in Shanghai have already done. I was, after all, a child when I lived there. My story is told from that perspective. I write of a personal journey: one that tells of life situations and circumstances. I want to educate and create a bridge to other generations.

Much of what I relate in these pages is based on the stories told to me by my parents. Within these pages from the time I was seven or eight years old the narrative is mostly mine. Historical data has been culled from various sources on public record. Unlike most survivors stories, my account of life in Shanghai encompasses both war and post-war years including the rise of Communism.

In 1996, I told my story to the Shoah Foundation who interviewed me in St. Catharines, ON. The foundation's purpose is to document a visual history of Jewish survivors of the Holocaust. In February 2001, I gave interviews for both the CBC Metro Morning Show and The St. Catharines Standard. It was after the Standard article and with the encouragement of many that I decided to commit my Shanghai memoir to paper.

Acknowledgements 安娜樂麗

I would like to express my gratitude to a number of people without whom this book would not have come to fruition.

To my dear husband, Velmer, who passed away just before this book was published. Thank you for the love, support, patience, and guidance. You will live in my heart forever. Thank you to my wonderful children, Paula and Michael, for your faith and continuous encouragement. To my brother Stephen Heinemann and his partner Fran Merion, thank you for lending a helping hand and refreshing my memory when needed.

I am deeply grateful to my good friend Helen Cannon, who instigated the writing of this book and graciously prodded me on when I felt like giving up: Professors Stella Slade and Barbara Bucknall, for their scholarly imput; Ernest and Illo Heppner, fellow Shanghai refugees and family friends, for sharing their memories; Manisha Solomon and Craig Bondy for bringing this book to fruition; Wil De Clercq, for his expertise to the redrafting of my original manuscript; and the many other friends, too many to mention, for their kindness and encouragement.

SURVIVORS OF THE
SHOAH
VISUAL HISTORY FOUNDATION™

13 October 1996

Hannelore Headley
71 Queen St.
St. Catharines, Ont. L2R 5G9
Canada

Dear Mrs. Headley,

In sharing your personal testimony as a survivor of the Holocaust, you have granted future generations the opportunity to experience a personal connection with history.

Your interview will be carefully preserved as an important part of the most comprehensive library of testimonies ever collected. Far into the future, people will be able to see a face, hear a voice, and observe a life, so that they may listen and learn, and always remember.

Thank you for your invaluable contribution, your strength, and your generosity of spirit.

MAIN OFFICE · POST OFFICE BOX 3168 · LOS ANGELES, CALIFORNIA 90078-3168 · PHONE 818.777-7802 FAX 818.733-0312

Contents 

1

Escape From Berlin

BEFORE AND AFTER KRISTALLNACHT

November 9, 1938, dawned as did most other days in Hitler's Germany. Before the day was over the lives of thousands of people would be forever changed. It would be a night of infamy and go down in history as Kristallnacht, the "Night of Broken Glass." I was just two-and-a-half years old when the madness of Kristallnacht was unleashed on my fellow Jews of Germany. Unlike others, I was sound asleep and mercifully oblivious to it all. Its repercussions, however, I was not able to escape. The fate of millions of Jews, including my family and myself was sealed that night. It was the beginning of the end.

Kristallnacht unfolded as one of the most horrific and shameful moments in Germany's history. That night, and well into the next day, hundreds of synagogues and thousands of Jewish businesses were destroyed in a frenzy of Nazi-inspired anti-Semitism. Other than to ensure that no looting of buildings took place, the country's police forces did nothing to curtail the violence and destruction. Firefighters were indifferent; their only concern was to protect German-owned buildings.

Hordes of spectators watched as vicious members of the dreaded Schutzstaffel (SS) and brainwashed Hitler

Youth, went on an unparalleled rampage. In addition to targeting businesses and places of worship, Jewish homes were vandalized. Jewish men were wantonly attacked and murdered; Jewish women and children were brutalized. At least ninety Jews were killed and some twenty-six thousand Jewish men were rounded up and shipped off to concentration camps. The destruction would resonate across the German Reich as a macabre symphony of splintering glass, the roar of burning buildings, and the screams of men, women, and children.

Kristallnacht would shake the very foundation of German society and send shockwaves throughout western civilization. Sadly, foreign governments would mostly ignore it. At best, the response was token protestations by lame politicians. These men either did not quite grasp the gravity of the situation, or they secretly harboured anti-Semitic sentiments themselves. For those German Jews who managed to hold on to a modicum of hope since that ignominious day the Nazis came to power, April 1, 1933, Kristallnacht was the definitive wake-up call.

The belief that Jews were living in a time of temporary madness, that their good German neighbours and friends would not stand by to let this horror go on, was now completely shattered along with the ruined and fire-gutted synagogues. After Kristallnacht, the number of Jews wishing to leave Germany increased dramatically. So did the awareness that anti-Semitic feelings, although less severe than those of Nazi Germany, was the consensus of many nations around the world. Jews simply were not welcome anywhere.

My father had already experienced, as early as 1936,

that leaving Germany was no walk in the park. But there seemed less urgency then. Kristallnacht changed things. Despite the fact that Mama and Papa kept their fears hidden from me, there was a certain desperation and tension in our home that was undeniable. Children can often feel their parents' anxiety with the same intensity that parents can feel that of their children. Despite my tender age, somehow I knew that my life was about to change forever.

I was a leap year baby. I was born in Berlin to Heinz-Egon Heinemann and Paula Kate Silberstein Heinemann on February 29, 1936. It was not a very auspicious year to be born a Jew in the German Reich. Many Jewish children would perish within the decade–never knowing the innocence of childhood, never growing into adulthood. But Mama, ever the one to interpret things as either a good or bad omen, deemed the date of my birth as the best of omens. "Our darling daughter will bring us luck," she declared. "She is a harbinger of good fortune."

At the time of my birth, Berlin was the largest city in Europe. It had a population of 4.3 million inhabitants, spread over an area of 880 square kilometres. The nation's capital was also the tenth largest Jewish centre in the

Hannelore with Mama, Papa, and Opa, 1936

world. Berlin's peak Jewish population of one hundred and seventy thousand residents had already started to dwindle by the time I first saw the light of day. It is shocking to note that as late as 1943, the last remaining Jews in Berlin, some ten thousand souls, would have been rounded up like cattle and sent to their deaths. Many had been in hiding; some had been successful at blending in with the rest of the German population. By the end of World War II, however, only a handful would remain in the city. Although I spent just a mere fraction of my life in Berlin, the great historic city would leave its mark on me.

Mama's side of the family was firmly rooted in the nation's capital. The Silberstein family moved to the city from Silesia in Eastern Prussia where for generations they were engaged in diverse trades including farming and that of licensed journeymen and carpenters.

My maternal grandparents, Heinrich Silberstein and Helene Schiftan Silberstein, however, were very much products of Berlin. They flourished there at the helm of their own businesses and were among the first of their respective lineages to venture away from the usual family occupations. Opa Silberstein was a successful haberdasher who, after working in various clothing stores to learn the trade, went on to operate his own men's apparel store. Helene was a very progressive woman and one of a rare breed of female entrepreneurs in the early decades of the twentieth century. She ran an equally successful domestic help agency. Her agency was a novel enterprise for its time, both in concept and gender ownership. It was still very much a man's world, and the notion of contracting out chefs, maids, butlers, cleaning personnel and other help on a per need basis was on the leading edge. Unfortunately, I never knew Helene, as she died from the complications of diabetes shortly before I was born. I would learn about her life through Opa's reminiscences. It is from her that I inherited the diabetes gene. Opa Silberstein, however, would play a pivotal role in my life, especially after we left Berlin.

Helene Schiftan Silberstein, Paula at age 7 (Hannelore's mother), Heinrich (Hannelore's Opa), and Berthold (Heinrich brother), 1917

The Silberstein's lives, like those of all Germans, underwent dramatic changes at the outbreak of World War I in 1914. When his country needed him, Opa, together with his brother, Berthold, immediately joined the army as volunteers. They served in the 52nd Infantry Regiment for more than four years and fought on both the Eastern and Western Fronts. Opa eventually became a sergeant and did further duty as the battalion's diarist. He and Berthold survived the war without injury, and Opa was awarded several medals including the Iron Cross. Like so many of his comrades who were also Jewish, he always thought of himself as being German. Two decades later, it would seem inconceivable to him that he would have to face the prospect of a concentration camp and imminent death at the hands of the very same people he had once fought to defend. This treachery would haunt him for the rest of his life.

My mother, Paula Kate, was born in 1910. As an only child, she was doted upon and felt very loved and cared for. She enjoyed the good life of an upper middle-class family and was encouraged in every way to pursue her interests, intellectual or otherwise.

She was a beautiful woman–not tall, but very distinctive with dark hair, piercing eyes, and chiselled features. Like her mother, Mama was a modern woman, blessed with a great intellect and passion for life.

As a child, her summers were spent at a family farm in Silesia. The rest of the year was spent in Berlin. Not all of Mama's childhood memories were pleasant in nature, however. Post-WWI Berlin was a city stung by inglorious defeat. Humiliation ran deep and seemed to affect everyone. Berlin, as the capital of the newly founded Weimar Republic, transformed into a city of paradoxes. Hyperinflation ruled the day, there were shortages of food, and unemployment was rampant. The cityscape of Berlin was coloured in shades of hope and despair, progress and regression, wealth and poverty.

Berlin of the 1920s and much of the 1930s, was a restless city. First it became the city of "Cabaret," a decadent city that revelled in its own recklessness. Still, Berlin continued to embody the Zeitgeist of Germany and was a powerful magnet for writers, artists, and musicians from all over the world. It was a city of intrigue and high drama. During the 1920s Berlin was also where the emerging Fascists clashed with Communists for the support of a disillusioned people. Social and political unrest affected every level of society. After the Fascists neutralized the Communists, they targeted the Weimar Republic for control of the country. Adolph Hitler, the dictator-in-waiting, would galvanize the Fascists into action. Finally, in 1933, Berlin became the nerve centre of the victorious Nazi regime's Third Reich. From then on, the city would spiral, ever so slowly, into the abyss that would lead to World War II and the Holocaust. This is the city of the Silbersteins and the Heinemanns. This is the city from which we would escape.

My father, Heinz-Egon Heinemann, was born in 1912 in Wiesbaden, a town not far from Frankfurt. He was a handsome, gregarious man with a sense of self-confidence that negated his shortness of stature. His parents, Richard Heinemann and Lotte Gumpel Heinemann, had divorced when Papa was just a youngster. He and his younger sister, Ellen, ceased to have contact with their mother for many years. When their father, Richard Heinemann, remarried, all three converted to the Lutheran faith of his second wife, Feodora von Buggenhagen. In keeping with the religious conversion, they were all baptized. It is with Feodora, who was of noble birth, that Papa established a loving and lasting relationship.

Richard Heinemann was a successful businessman whose fortunes waned and waxed with the erratic times.

Feodora, Richard, Heinz-Egon (Hannelore's Papa), and Ellen (Hannelore's aunt), 1921

Paternal great-grandmother Erna Gumpel with Hannelore at the Würtzburgerstraße apartment, c. 1938

During WWI he owned a canning factory that had a contract to supply canned rations to German troops. This business came to an end after the war. A man of many talents, Richard Heinemann landed the job of estate administrator for the von Lippe-Biesterfeld family.

Although considered middle class on the social register, the Heinemanns enjoyed a high standard of living and mixed with German nobility of the era. Like Mama, Papa enjoyed a privileged upbringing. He spent his formative years on an estate belonging to the von Lippe-Biesterfelds. Papa grew up with and befriended one of the von Lippe-Biesterfeld heirs, Prince Bernhard, who would eventually marry Queen Juliana of the Netherlands. When not cavorting with the prince, Papa spent much of his time in the estate's huge library. He was mesmerized by the diverse collection of books, many of them being centuries old. Papa read voraciously and developed not only a lifelong passion for precious books but also for Flemish and Dutch art history of the sixteenth and seventeenth centuries.

Eventually, the Heinemann family moved to Berlin. Although they prospered for a number of years in various business enterprises, tragedy befell Richard Heinemann. After losing all his business interests in the declining economic times that afflicted Germany, compounded by the infamous stock market crash of 1929, he took his own life.

After completing his high school studies, Papa pursued his interest in books and became an apprentice to S. Martin Fraenkel, a well-known Berlin book dealer. As an employee, Papa was frequently sent to libraries to borrow intact copies of rare and expensive books. Mr. Fraenkel eventually became notorious in book circles for his fondness of surreptitiously removing pages and illustrations out of these books. He would insert these pages into identical books that were missing those plates in order to be able to sell them at full value. This odious practice is still known in the used and rare book industry as "frankeling." Papa, who treated books as if they were precious jewels, was never able to come to terms with his mentor's practices. After completing his apprenticeship, he quickly left the employ of Mr. Fraenkel. Shortly, thereafter, Papa was able to acquire a position as an art historian with the National Kunst Museum in Berlin. He worked in the Kupferkabinett, specializing in Flemish and Dutch art. Papa also became one of the youngest contributors to Welt Kunst, a prestigious art magazine. Throughout his employment with the museum, his love of fine books continued to be closest to his heart.

Early in 1933, at the age of 21, Papa opened his own

shop aptly known as Oliva Buchhandlung, as it was located on the Oliva Platz. He quickly established himself as one of the more popular book dealers in Berlin, counting among his many well-known clients the Papal Nuncio Eugenio Pacelli who, in 1939, would become Pope Pius XII. With Oliva Buchhandlung, Papa had truly found his niche; he would remain a book dealer for the rest of his life. Perhaps it was inevitable because his love for books had been passed down to him from the family gene pool. Papa took after William Heinemann, his grandfather's brother, who founded the London, England, publishing house William Heinemann Ltd., years earlier. The company had gained prominence as a publishing house of distinction, working with authors such as Somerset Maugham, Joseph Conrad, and J.B. Priestley to name a few. Although no longer in my family, the company still exists today.

In addition to sustaining his love for books, Oliva Buchhandlung led to another love affair for Papa. This one was with a dentistry student named Paula Silberstein. After high school, Mama had chosen to enter the medical profession. When it became clear that under Hitler she would not be able to complete her degree, she switched to dentistry. Being an avid reader and book collector, Mama had heard from friends about the new book haven and its charming young owner on the Oliva Platz. She knew she had to investigate the store and, of course, the much talked about proprietor.

At the time, Mama was engaged to Dr. Heinz Behrend, a practicing dentist, with whom she shared a fascination for the paranormal. Although taking up a romance with a book dealer was the furthest thing from her mind, she was unable to resist Mr. Heinemann's charm and fell head-over-heels in love with him. Although Papa did not share Mama's avid, lifelong interest in the paranormal, he did share her enthusiasm for the Berlin nightlife and social scene. They frequented the city's many cabarets and went to concerts, the theatre, and the cinema. They attended art gallery openings and poetry readings, and their combined circle of eclectic friends ensured that there were plenty of parties and social gatherings to attend.

After a whirlwind courtship, Mama and Papa were married in 1934. They moved into a spacious second floor apartment, located in a four-plex building with a concierge on the Würtzburgerstraße, not far from the centre of town. The newlyweds filled their apartment with fine furnishings, paintings, sculptures, and books of every description. Despite their happiness and comfortable lifestyle, the ominous shadow Hitler and his anti-Semitic minions were casting over Germany was one they were unable to ignore. Mama was beginning to realize that even though she would be able to complete her dentistry studies, her chances of opening a practice under the new regime were next to zero. The Nazi boycott of Jewish professionals was, indeed, soon to become a reality.

On April 1, 1933, the day the Nazis came to power, a simple but malicious one-day boycott of Jewish-owned shops was proclaimed. To ensure the boycott achieved its intended goal, members of the Sturm Abteilung (SA), better known as "storm troopers" or "brown shirts," were dispersed to picket designated shops all over the country. Soon, "Achtung Juden" and the Star of David were graffitied on Jewish businesses all over Germany to set these establishments apart from "Aryan concerns." Hitler's early strategy for oppression was to make life so unpleasant for Jews that they would choose to emigrate en masse to other countries. What the Führer had not taken into account was that German Jews considered themselves as much children of the Fatherland as the Aryans did. Many traced their roots in the country back to the Middle Ages. Many had had fought in its wars, some as recently as WWI.

Unlike Jewish communities in Eastern Europe, Jews in pre-war Germany were fully integrated at all levels of German life and society. Although no strangers to anti-Semitism from some segments of the population, Jews were stunned by the Nazi's philosophical line of thought and were totally unprepared for what was to come. They did not take up arms to defend themselves, believing that the madness would go away. Still, there were those who took heed and left the country. It was a trickle at first, but as anti-Semitism increased year by year, so did the number of exits. It has since been estimated that close to two hundred and fifty thousand Jews, approximately half the Jewish population of Germany, emigrated between 1933 and 1939.

For Papa, the longevity of his newly opened bookstore looked equally gloomy, especially after May 10, 1933. On that day, the Nazis perpetrated one of the most despicable acts imaginable to Papa–the mass destruction of books. Pro-Nazi student organizations, professors, and librarians had secretly drawn up long lists of books considered unfit to be read by the German public. Books by Jewish, left wing, and modernist authors were unceremoniously thrown into roaring bonfires by members of the SA at the Opernplatz in Berlin and in many other university towns across Germany. Even books by such American authors as Helen Keller, Margaret Sanger, Upton Sinclair, and Ernest Hemingway were burned.

Following the burnings, many German writers and intellectuals, both Jewish and Aryan, fled in significant numbers to England, France, and the United States. Not even Helen Keller's response to the burnings that "tyranny cannot defeat the power of ideas," would placate Papa. He was totally beside himself. "It is an outrage against humanity what they have done. Those who burn books will not hesitate to burn the authors," Papa told Mama about what he had witnessed.

The Hitler adoration that swept through Germany at this time became hard to ignore. In 1934, Mama's intellectual curiosity regarding the Hitler phenomenon got the better of her; she decided to attend a Nazi rally in Berlin. Although this rally paled in comparison to the gigantic Nuremburg Party Rallies, Mama was deeply affected by the cleverly organized fanfare that day. She confessed later that the hysterical response of the participants was mesmerizing. "I had to remain aloof by reminding myself who I was and why I was there. I came away with a renewed sense of foreboding and a better understanding of why it had become so easy for the ordinary person to subscribe to the escalating anti-Semitic outrages that were sweeping the country," Mama told me years later.

In 1935, at the Nazi Party Rally in Nuremburg, the infamous "Nuremberg Laws" were enacted. The laws were meant to be a decisive and irrevocable escalation in the persecution of Jews; ultimately these laws would result in the Holocaust. The anti-Semitic scenario scripted by the Nazis had been a work in progress, spreading like a plague from one part of the country to the other, city by city, and village by village. Hostility towards Jews increased exponentially with the rumours, innuendos, disinformation, and new decrees. Many German business owners, brainwashed by daily doses of anti-Semitic propaganda, took it upon themselves not to serve the Jewish population. Signs declaring "No admittance to Jews" and "Jews enter these premises at their own risk" began to appear all over Germany.

The next step in the segregation was the German boycotting of Jewish professionals, including doctors, dentists, and lawyers. SA henchmen put pressure on ordinary citizens not to buy goods produced by Jewish companies. Those who did were subjected to intimidation and labelled "Jew lovers." Jewish civil servants, teachers, and those employed by the media were systematically fired from their jobs. Jewish-controlled media companies were forced to liquidate or sell their assets. Many of the Jews who left Germany at this time did so because they could no longer earn a living. The number of Jews emigrating escalated after the Nuremberg Laws had been enacted. Under these new laws, Jews could no longer be considered citizens of Germany. With the same stroke of the pen, it became illegal for Jews to marry Aryans. Even the most optimistic of Jews had to concede that an air of sullen uncertainty hung over them. Eventually, Jews everywhere were barred from using public transportation, public buildings, parks, swimming pools, resorts, beaches, schools, and even hospitals.

The long-feared end to Papa's ownership of Oliva Buchhandlung became a reality in July 1936. He received a letter from the Prussian Secret Police, ordering him to close his bookstore. According to the official who had written the letter, Papa was dealing in written and printed materials contrary to the spirit of Nazi Germany. With a heavy heart Papa complied. He knew he had no choice. If he did not close the store, the authorities would do it for him and in the process arrest him for sedition. Although devastated, Papa saw this turn of events coming and prepared himself accordingly. He wisely liquidated as many of the most valuable books in his inventory as possible.

Oliva Buchhandlung, Berlin

Heinz-Egon Heinemann, November 1933

Preußische Geheime Staatspolizei
Staatspolizeistelle für den Landespolizeibezirk Berlin

Berlin C 25, Alexanderstr. 10 und Grunerstr. 12
Ecke Dircksenstraße

Eingangs- und Bearbeitungsvermerk

An die
Oliva-Buchhandlung
z.Hd.v.Herrn Heinz
H e i n e m a n n ,
Berlin-Schöneberg,
Würzburger Str.18.

Geschäftszeichen und Tag Ihres Schreibens

Geschäftszeichen und Tag meines Schreibens
Stapo 6 3600 173/36
den 3. Juli 1936.

Betrifft:

Hiermit wird die am 27.6.1936 auf Grund der Verordnung des Herrn Reichspräsidenten zum Schutze von Volk und Staat vom 28.2.1933 erfolgte polizeiliche Schliessung Ihrer in Berlin W.15, Lietzenburger Strasse 24/25, gelegenen Buchhandlung bestätigt. Gleichzeitig wird der gesamte Bücherbestand polizeilich beschlagnahmt und sichergestellt.

Die Schliessung erfolgt , weil Sie bis in die jüngste Zeit hinein in bedeutendem Umfange Bücher mit politisch und kulturell zersetzender Tendenz vertrieben haben. Diese Sabotage der nationalsozialistischen Aufbauarbeit auf dem Gebiet des deutschen Schrifttums stellt zugleich eine erhebliche Gefährdung der Staatssicherheit dar, in deren Interesse der ständige Vertrieb zersetzender Schriften durch eine Buchhandlung nicht geduldet werden kann.

Fernerhin untersage ich Ihnen jede weitere buchhändlerische Betätigung.

Im Auftrage:
gez. Dr. Albath.

Polizeipräsident für den Landespolizeibezirk Berlin Staatspolizeistelle

Beglaubigt.

Heftrand

Din A 4
210×297 mm
Vordruck
Pol. Nr. 2

.........Anlagen

Fernruf
Berlin
E 1 Berolina 0023

Postscheckkonto
Berlin 2386
Kasse
des Geheimen Staatspolizeiamts

Fi

Prussian Secret Police of the State letter, July 3, 1936 (original)

P r u s s i a n S e c r e t P o l i c e o f t h e S t a t e .

State Police Department for the Police District Berlin.

Berlin C 25 Alexanderstr.lo und Grunerstr.12
Ecke Dirksenstrasse.

To the
" O l i v a " Book -Shop
Attention: Mr. Heinz H e i n e m a n n ,
Berlin - Schöneberg
Würzburgerstr.18

S T A P O 6 3600 173/36
den 3. Juli 1936.

This is to certify that on account of the decree of the State Police President for the protection of People and State your book - shop,situated at Berlin,W.15, Lietzenburger-Strasse 24/25 has been closed. At the same time the entire stock of books will be seized by the police and secured.

The shop has been closed, because you have sold a great deal of books up to the last moment,the contents of which were of politically and culturally decomposing tendency. This sabotage of the constructive work of National-Socialism concerning the German literature is at the same time a great threat to the State security,in whose interest the constant sale of decomposing literature by a book - shop can not be tolerated.

Moreover I forbid you any further book = selling activity.

By order :
signed: Dr. Albath .

Verified.
Signature. Seal.

This is to certify that the above is a true copy - translation of the original document.

Shanghai, December 8, 1948

Dr. Max Steingraber, Chairman.

Prussian Secret Police of the State letter, July 3, 1936 (translation)

Shortly following this directive, the store reopened under new non-Jewish ownership. The substitute proprietor, who knew nothing about books and was just trying to be a good German citizen, regularly consulted Papa for his expertise. This consultation was in the strictest confidence, as it would run afoul of the Nazi laws if the arrangement became known. Papa was happy to oblige and was paid much needed income in exchange for his invaluable knowledge.

The loss of Oliva Buchhandlung prompted Papa to take a trip to South Africa to see what possibilities might be open for us as immigrants. The prospects seemed favourable, and he returned home to prepare for the move. On the day Papa went to apply, he found, much to his dismay, that South Africa had joined the many other countries that now denied entry to Jewish refugees.

Shortly after this major disappointment, Mama and Papa found themselves duped by a passport scheme. The con resulted in a huge scandal, and many people lost their savings. Fortunately, Papa was able to retrieve his money, some 12,000 Deutsche marks in total. It was a cold comfort, however, knowing that our fates would be sealed if we were unable to leave an ever-maddening Germany. As the situation worsened, particularly after the events of Kristallnacht, Mama and Papa, like so many other desperate people, were now willing to go almost anywhere the doors were still open. One such place was Shanghai, China, which ended up accepting more Jewish refugees than the combined total of those taken in by Canada, Australia, New Zealand, South Africa, and India.

At the time, one could still leave Germany with an exit permit, which was good for three months from the day of issue. The permit came with a caveat, however. If the permit was allowed to expire, one risked almost certain arrest. Although Kristallnacht had thoroughly convinced Mama and Papa that it was high time to leave the country, they were particularly anxious to depart after two major incidents suddenly befell the Silberstein family. The first of which was when one of Oma Silberstein's cousins, Georg Fabilch was involved in a bicycle accident on a Berlin street and arrested at once by the police. A week later, his wife, Erna, was summoned to the police station and unceremoniously handed a shoebox containing her husband's belongings. Amongst the items were his eyeglasses, which were broken and showed evidence of dried blood. No information or explanation was given; the 38-year-old father of three was never heard of or seen again.

Am 28. Juli 1938 entschlief plötzlich mein geliebter Mann, unser guter Vater, Sohn, Bruder und Freund

Georg Fabisch

im 38. Lebensjahr.

In tiefer Trauer

Erna Fabisch, geb. Kuske
Harry Fabisch
Max Fabisch
Frieda Fabisch

Berlin W 62, Lützowplatz 16

Die Urnenbeisetzung findet am Sonntag, dem 14. August 11 Uhr, Weißensee, Neue Halle, statt.

Death announcement for Georg Fabilch, July 28, 1938

The second incident happened a few months later when Opa received a visit from a former comrade-at-arms. This man, who was not Jewish, came in the middle of the night with a dire warning. He was a civil servant with access to certain documents, one being a list of Jews who had fought in WWI. "My dear friend, I come with bad news. I have seen your name on a Gestapo list, and that can only mean one thing in these wretched times. You must hide yourself and try to get out of Germany as quickly as possible," the man told him. Opa reacted with disbelief, certain that his old army friend was mistaken. "But I am a law-abiding citizen who has honourably served Germany during the war. This is preposterous! There must be a mistake," is all he could say. The friend assured Opa that the list was for real and urged him to take the matter seriously. "I could be severely reprimanded if it was known I warned you. You must take precautions and try to get out of the country as soon as possible," the man reiterated as he took his leave. Opa still had trouble accepting the fact that such a betrayal of German Jews was possible and mulled over his friend's advice. Not long afterwards, however, the warning took on a totally new meaning: the events of Kristallnacht! The reality of this terrible night convinced not only Opa to go into hiding, but Papa as well. They bid Mama a hasty farewell and went into hiding immediately. It proved to be a wise decision.

A little later, two Gestapo agents appeared at our door demanding to take Opa and Papa into custody. Mama told them that they had left, expecting the agents to barge into the apartment and see for themselves. For some reason they chose not to pursue the matter and went on their way.

The following night, the same Gestapo agents returned to have another look but the apartment building concierge, Frau Mueller, stopped them in the hallway. Frau Mueller, a non-Jew, was a fearless elderly lady and very matronly in appearance. She had no use for Nazi henchmen and chose to confront them. "Herr Heinemann and Herr Silberstein no longer live here. Take my word for it. Only his wife and daughter remain. Why do you two want to disturb a young woman and her two-year-old child? Surely they are not a threat to the Reich," she protested. Thankfully, the men turned and left. If they had not, this would have been a much different story; one that perhaps would have never been told. Over the years, Mama often recounted the heroics of brave Frau Mueller that night. "I dare not think what would have happened if she hadn't stuck her neck out for us like that. People like Frau Mueller were proof positive that not everybody in Germany was anti-Semitic, and some did care about other human beings," she said.

Despite the dangers of being in public, Papa joined the hundreds of Jews queuing up at the travel offices of Thomas Cook. He did this on a daily basis, standing in line for hours on end in all kinds of weather. His objective was to buy tickets to Shanghai. Like most of the other hopefuls, he found the quest to obtain tickets to freedom frustrating and largely unsuccessful. Papa became more and more discouraged as the long days evaporated into even longer weeks. He feared that the Heinemann family was destined to remain in Germany, their future uncertain and totally at the mercy of the unpredictable Nazis.

One dismal day, while travelling on a crowded Berlin tram to the offices of Thomas Cook, Papa encountered former bookshop client Herr Kohn. "I'm afraid my wife's mother has fallen ill, Herr Heinemann. We have to cancel our departure to Shanghai. But perhaps it was meant to be, our remaining in Germany. Surely order will be restored," he told Papa. Although Papa did not share this delusion, he knew that many other Jews, despite the gravity of the recent Kristallnacht, shared his acquaintance's line of thought. He asked Herr Kohn how many tickets he was returning and was informed that there were four. "But that is exactly the number I wish to acquire," he blurted, trying hard to curb his excitement. "At the risk of sounding like an opportunist, Herr Kohn, would you mind if I accompanied you to see if I can purchase them?" Mr. Kohn agreed and told Papa he would be a fool not to act upon the opportunity. They proceeded to the travel agency together: one with the hope that he would get a refund on the tickets, the other that he would be able to buy them.

Papa did his utmost to control the anxiety that gripped him as they joined the usual lengthy line-up at Thomas Cook. The tickets he so desperately needed to assure his family's freedom were suddenly within reach; but would he be able to obtain them? The question burned in his mind for what seemed like an eternity, coupled with the guilt that his family stood to benefit from another family's misfortune. When they finally reached the service counter they faced a jaded and, no doubt, overworked clerk. As it turned out, Herr Kohn had no problem returning the tickets and getting back his money. Papa, however, was informed that it was not a simple matter of just transferring the tickets from one family to another. He quickly ascertained that what the clerk meant was that he would gladly accept some kind of compensation to facilitate the transaction. Fortunately, Papa had a sufficient amount of cash with him. He bribed the clerk and walked out of the office elated, with tickets in hand.

I was already in bed, although not asleep, when he came home that evening with the tickets. I heard him and called to him, longing for a hug and a goodnight kiss. He and Mama came into my room seeming more at ease than I had ever seen them. "Hello, my darling Hannelore," Papa said. "We are going to go on a long trip, you, me, Mama, and Opa." He smiled happily, picked me up off my bed, and held me tight. For the first time in weeks I saw what looked like a glimmer in his eyes. It was by sheer fluke that we would be able to make good our escape from Germany. "Fate deals many cards and comes in many guises. In this instance it smiles upon us," Mama told Papa in all her wisdom. "It is best not to question its intentions." He knew that she was right. The circumstance of how our escape came about would stay with Papa for the rest of his life. He would often wonder what happened to the hapless Herr Kohn and his family. Perhaps it is best he never found out, as the Kohns were never heard from again after that fateful day at Thomas Cook.

As in all Jewish departures from Germany, one had to forfeit his or her citizenship and thus become a stateless refugee. One did not simply pack up and go; that would have been too easy in a country where everything had become so very complicated. One also had to submit to a thorough police inspection of the goods that were to be taken out of the country. All valuables were to be left behind. These goods were then destined for auction or private sales, with the proceeds going to the Nazi party coffers. Not surprisingly, fine works of art, antiques, and expensive jewellery found their way into the possession of the party hierarchy instead. Papa had managed to liquidate most of the precious books, works of art, and objects of value from our home in anticipation that the day would come that we might lose everything.

Now that my family, the Heinemanns, were finally in a legal position to leave the country, Opa returned to the Würtzburgerstraße apartment to help Mama pack. Clothing, personal items, and basic household goods were just about the only items allowed out of the country. Somehow, we were given permission to take our large dining table. In keeping with the law, Mama notified the local police precinct that we were packing in order to leave the country. Two constables were sent to supervise the proceedings. In a scene straight out of a B-movie comedy, while Mama and Papa hid whatever valuables they still owned, Opa kept the constables sufficiently distracted with jokes and party tricks–and a good bottle of schnapps! When the suitcases and shipping trunk were stuffed to the maximum, the slightly inebriated constables gave the contents a cursory glance and then put the official seal on them. It was a done deal; we were ready to leave Berlin.

Our tickets to freedom were issued for an Italian liner named the S.S. *Julio César*. The port of departure was Genoa, Italy. Demand upon ships to provide passage to the Orient was so great that Italian shipping lines had seized the opportunity to run a shuttle service between Genoa and Shanghai. The ships carried thousands of passengers, who took up every available foot of space on the lucrative route to the East. We were scheduled to sail on April 15, 1939; six years had gone by since the Nazis had come to power and embarked upon their mission to rid Germany of Jews. Mama and Papa were relieved that our final departure from the madness of Hitler's totalitarian regime was at hand; yet they were equally distressed about leaving Berlin. For Opa, leaving Berlin was an especially traumatic prospect: not so much because it was his home, but that it was the burial place of his beloved wife Helene. Although her memory was imbedded in his heart, he feared her grave would fall into ruin once he could no longer tend it.

Being a three-year-old, I, of course, did not share all this consternation. All I knew was that we were going on a long trip. I did not understand that we were leaving our home, not by design but out of necessity. Only much later did I grasp that we were among the relatively few lucky families to have obtained passage out of Germany. How many thousands of others might have enjoyed the same good fortune if world governments had opened their doors to a desperate and doomed people? With WWII looming on the horizon, it had become impossible to enter any South American country, Canada, or the United States. No country in Africa offered safe haven, either. Even though England had arranged for many Austrian and German Jewish children to be rescued in an operation known as "Kinder Transport," it turned out to be just a drop in the ocean compared to those who would perish. Furthermore, as an adult, one was required to have at least £1,000 and a high professional profile to enter the United

Kingdom. To enter Palestine, the beloved Jewish homeland, which was still under British mandate in 1939, at least £500 was required; and still it was difficult to cut through the red tape.

Though Hitler and his cohorts perpetrated the Holocaust, all those countries that turned a blind eye towards the European Jews were also guilty. China, on the other hand, did not raise any objections to large-scale Jewish immigration. As a result some 22,000 Jews would find refuge there, but only in the International Settlement port of Shanghai. This area ironically, was occupied by Japan, an imperialistic nation friendly with Germany. Why the Japanese facilitated the entrance of Jews into Shanghai was unclear at the time. It was not something those fortunate enough to find shelter there questioned. Later, it was rumoured that the Sassoons and the Kadoories, wealthy long-time Jewish residents of Shanghai, had negotiated a business deal with the Japanese. The occupying Japanese had, no doubt, considered it in their best interest to maintain normal economic and commercial activities in Shanghai. Whatever the reasons, the only thing that truly mattered was that this faraway city of the Orient offered a haven to a desperate people.

Getting from Berlin to Genoa was a major undertaking in 1939. Mama and Papa had decided that the easiest way to travel from Germany to Italy was by train. Because Jews were allowed to take only a limited amount of money out of the country, which was next to useless outside of Germany anyway, Papa had purchased "first–class" tickets for the journey. We may have been stateless refugees fleeing Germany, but we were fleeing in style.

It was late afternoon as the four of us boarded the train at Berlin's Hauptbahnhof in early April. Not all was well in the cavernous train station, as it was cloaked in an atmosphere of anxiety. There was the usual frenetic activity of people coming and going, but there was not the usual tears of departure or joy of arrival. Nazi officials had also boarded our train in order to recheck everyone's documents, despite the fact that the passengers had already been duly processed. There was some commotion as a number of older men were hustled from the train. It became obvious to us that there was a lookout for men over a certain age. Opa believed, rightly or wrongly, that the officials were looking for Jewish WWI veterans and he decided to get off the train. He bid us a quick farewell and tried to assure Mama, who was very distraught by what was happening, that he would take a later train and rendezvous with us in Genoa. Mama feared that she would never see him again, yet she also knew it was not the time or place for histrionics. Meanwhile, I did not understand why Opa was leaving us when he was supposed to be going with us. My eager questions as to this change in plans went unanswered.

We watched Opa slip off the train, just steps ahead of the men inspecting the passengers' visas and tickets. As if the incident with Opa was not unnerving enough, another moment of extreme dread seized Mama and Papa before the train left the station; they believed it was all over for us. We had just settled into our luxurious seats when the compartment's door suddenly hissed open. Standing in the portal was an SS officer. His presence was starkly defined by a finely tailored midnight black uniform, knee-high riding boots, and a peaked cap prominently displaying the ominous death's head. He struck a most sinister figure.

To the relief of Mama and Papa it became quickly evident that he was not on the train to arrest us. While he appraised us with detached interest, he introduced himself and informed us he was taking the train to the Swiss border and would be sharing our compartment. Seeing a well-dressed blonde, blue-eyed German family travelling first class did not seem to lead him to suspect that we were Jewish. Mama and Papa's cool and calm demeanour suggested anything but the fact that we were fleeing the country. My gregarious behaviour seemed to be a pleasant distraction for all. A conversation ensued between the officer and Mama and Papa as the train made its way to the Swiss border. The black-clad man even dangled me on his knee and prophesised that I would one day be a great leader of German women. How ironic this sentiment must have seemed to Mama and Papa: their little Jewish daughter a poster child for the future of a glorious Aryan Germany. After reaching the Swiss border, the SS officer rose from his seat, clicked his heels, bowed farewell, and disembarked the train. I am certain that Mama and Papa breathed a sigh of relief when he was gone.

Our train continued through the spectacular Alps, the grandeur of which totally mesmerized me. After what seemed like forever, we finally reached our destination. Upon our arrival in Genoa, Papa rented a small room for us. We still had a week left before sailing to Shanghai. It was a time of great anxiety as we awaited the arrival of Opa. No doubt, my continuous inquiries as to Opa's whereabouts exacerbated an already tense situation. Mama religiously made the daily journey to the train station to greet him, and became increasingly agitated when day after day he failed to appear. From one such fruitless trip she arrived back at the room, reduced to tears. "We are leaving in a few days and Papa still isn't here. Something has happened to him, Heinz. I know it. He has been arrested. I'm never going to see him again," she said between sobs. Papa did his best to comfort her, but deep down he probably feared she was right.

The next day, less than twenty-four hours before our departure time on the *Julio César*, Mama returned once more without Opa. She was visibly overcome with grief. Then, as suddenly as Opa had disappeared from the train in Berlin, he appeared at our room door. He looked tired, his suit was rumpled, and he sported a bit of stubble on his face. It was unusual for Opa not to shave and dress immaculately, as he always took the utmost pride in his appearance. "What's all the crying about?" he said with a smile. "Is that any way to welcome an old man?" Apparently he and Mama had missed each other at the station. He had arrived by an earlier train that day, and he had lost his way trying to find the place in which we were staying. When Mama asked him how he had managed to find us, he just winked, as if it was a matter of course he would find his family. Mama joyously threw herself into his open arms and embraced him. I, too, rushed to him and grabbed his leg; he picked me up and hugged me tightly. I felt like I was in heaven; my Opa had come back to me! It was a joyous reunion, and the anxiety we had felt earlier gave way to the excitement of our departure for Shanghai. There was little time left, and we quickly packed up to go to the dock. In just a few hours we would embark upon our journey into the unknown. Mama, Papa, and I would not set foot in Europe again for many years; Opa was destined never to return.

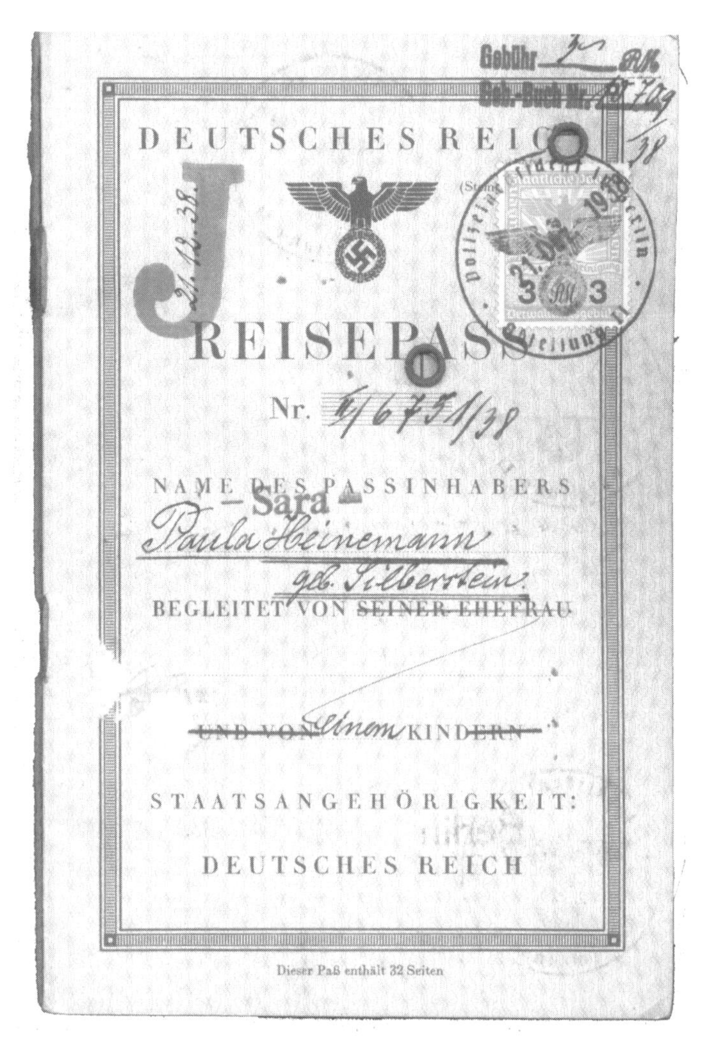
DEUTSCHES REICH

J

REISEPASS

Nr. 6751/38

NAME DES PASSINHABERS

Sara

Paula Heinemann

geb. Silberstein

BEGLEITET VON ~~SEINER EHEFRAU~~

~~UND VON~~ einem KIND~~ERN~~

STAATSANGEHÖRIGKEIT:

DEUTSCHES REICH

Dieser Paß enthält 32 Seiten

"J" for Jew. First page of Paula Silberstein Heinemann's travel pass

THE VOYAGE TO SHANGHAI

安娜樂麗

It was a beautiful spring day on April 20, 1939. The sun shone and there was a light breeze. There were a few clouds in the sky, but they were not threatening. "It is a good day to start a journey," Opa said as if he were a seasoned traveller. We made our way by taxi to the harbour, where there were many ships tied to their wharfs. Flocks of seagulls flew off under protest as we drove towards our ship's berth, only landing again when we had gone past them. There was activity everywhere in the harbour. The crew of the *Julio César* was in the midst of final preparations for the four-week-long trip to the Orient.

We came to a stop not far from the *Julio César's* dock and piled out of the taxi. There seemed to be a bit of a haggle over the taxi fare as Papa settled with the driver, but it ended to everyone's satisfaction. We grabbed our luggage and walked up to the gangplank of the magnificent ship. I had my own suitcase; it was very small and I carried it with pride. It contained a few of my favourite treasures such as my dolly, Lisa, and stuffed lion, Zoltar, which Opa had bought for me at the Berlin Zoo. I took a deep breath as we laboured up the long, steep gangplank of our freedom ship. I had never seen a ship before and its size overwhelmed me. Ever since leaving Berlin, everything had taken on gigantic proportions, starting with the train station and then the Alps. It was all new to me; I found it most stimulating and could not wait to get aboard the ship to sail into a glorious adventure.

The *Julio César* was one of the many luxury passenger liners that plied the Genoa to Shanghai refugee route of the late 1930s. She belonged to a golden era of vessels built during the early decades of the twentieth century: sleek, fast, and comfortable. She even had a swimming pool. But the latter was the least of her features that interested me. In keeping with our first–class train trip out of Germany, we were going first class the rest of the way to our new life. This was not a case of my parents putting on the Ritz, but it was one of spending as much of their German currency as possible. The last of our money including that which was recovered from the passport fiasco, was spent on making sure that the thirteen-thousand-kilometre journey to the Far East was a comfortable one.

Trip to Shanghai on the S.S. Julio César, April 20-May 15, 1939
Unidentified, Papa, Mama, Hannelore

After we stepped onto the ship, we announced ourselves to an uniformed reception officer, who looked a lot less threatening than the uniformed man on the train. A most friendly steward then escorted us to our cabin. While he pushed our luggage ahead of him on a trolley, he chattered away in a language none of us understood. I did not give him my suitcase, however. I wanted to make sure it did not get lost. It seemed to take forever to get to our cabin as we traversed long, narrow gangways that were lit by pretty frosted lights mounted on the bulkheads. "Here we are, Signor and Signora Heinemann and Signor Silberstein," the steward said at last in an effort to speak German. He brought us to a stop in front of a cabin door which he opened with a key, and then ushered us into a very nice and airy cabin. The steward gave Papa a set of keys and the three men then removed our luggage from the trolley. Papa slipped the steward a tip and the grateful crewmember told us to call him anytime we needed assistance. "Have a very nice voyage," he said as he pushed the trolley out of the cabin.

Now that we had been to our cabin and our luggage was safely stored, we went back on deck–but not before I retrieved Zoltar out of my suitcase! We found our way to one of the upper decks so we could have our last glimpse of Europe. I begged Mama to hoist me in her arms so I could have a bird's eye view of the activity below. Then there was a short, piercing blast from a horn somewhere up above, startling me. Opa explained the sound meant the ship was ready to leave and was a signal to cast off. And he was right because far below us gritty looking dock-labourers wearing greasy leather gloves slipped the ship's mooring lines from their bollards. Suddenly there were vibrations beneath our feet as the *Julio César* came to life. Without further ado or fanfare, the ship slowly inched away from the dock.

It seemed fitting that we were leaving the continent from this historic seaport, birthplace of such renowned explorers as Christopher Columbus and John Cabot. It was a port from which they sailed many times as young seamen. Later in life, I sometimes wondered if the spirit of these brave explorers had somehow been imparted into me. From the moment we had left port, an unquenchable thirst for adventure and exploration ebbed within me, much to the chagrin of my dear Mama.

There were no friends or family on the dock waving goodbye to the passengers onboard the ship. And from this point on, fewer and fewer of our fellow Jews would be able to make an exit out of Germany. I did not realize it at the time, but without a doubt this voyage was saving my life and that of Mama, Papa, and Opa. Less than a month before, things had been so desperate for my family as Papa sought to make arrangements for this precise moment. I felt a sense of relief emanating from Mama, Papa, and Opa, although they also looked a little sad. Still, there was a much more relaxed feeling now, as if a heavy weight had been cast from their shoulders.

"Come on sweetheart, it is time for your nap," Mama reminded me. "But I'm not tired," I protested as usual. Papa and Opa stayed on deck as Mama whisked me away. She had a bit of trouble finding our cabin again. I thought the search for it was fun because it was like a game of hide-and-seek, with the gangways acting like a maze. We found our cabin at last, and Mama tucked me into the bottom of one of the two, double-tiered bunk beds. My eyelids soon felt heavy, and I fell asleep with Zoltar cradled in my arms.

Over the next few days we all slipped into a leisurely shipboard routine as we effortlessly made our way through the azure waters of the Mediterranean, the sun-broiled Suez Canal, and the stifling Red Sea. There was a brief stopover in exotic Colombo, Ceylon, before we embarked on the final and most lengthy leg of our journey. Fortunately, we had good weather all the way to Shanghai, so nobody got seasick. Mama was relieved; being seasick was one of her pre-departure concerns. Yet what should have been a fairly uneventful journey turned out to be rather stressful for Mama and Papa. They did not realize what a shipboard terror a three-year-old could be. Mama would be fond of saying years later that I "walked all the way from Genoa to Shanghai," as I was all over the ship from stern to bow. I was determined, quite fearlessly, to discover every nook and cranny of my temporary floating home. This activity gave my frazzled parents very little respite.

Early into the voyage, one of my adventures sparked a severe panic attack in Mama and Papa. They feared I had gone missing. When they could not find me in any of my usual haunts, they thought that I had fallen overboard and was swallowed up by the sea. Papa anxiously notified the first steward he came across that his daughter was missing, and a general alarm was sent resonating throughout the ship. For many years I would have to hear about the frantic search that was conducted for me that day, with everyone hoping against the worst. I heard the alarm being raised but had no idea it was because of me. I had made my way down into the bowels of the ship, on narrow stairwells and catwalks. The oppressive heat and the grime of the boiler room did not bother me in the least. Moreover, the huge, pounding pistons of the gigantic steam engine fascinated me.

My exploratory tour of the engine room finally ended when some sweaty men in oil-stained coveralls spotted me. They could not believe their eyes when they saw me roaming around their domain. One of the men, who appeared to be cleaner than the rest, approached me and shouted something over the clattering noise of the engine. I gave him a frightened look because I did not know what he was yelling. I thought I was really in for it. Realizing my state of dread, he made an upward gesture indicating that he was going to take me back up on deck. He picked me up and, a few minutes later, the bemused engine room worker arrived on deck with me in his arms. We were greeted by applause from passengers and crew members.

I wondered what all the fuss was about and failed to understand why so many people were on deck. When I saw Mama, Papa, Opa, and the captain in the crowd, it became obvious that it had to do with me. The captain did not look amused; he did not applaud. He stood with his arms crossed, feet slightly apart, and gave me a stern look. Papa, Mama, and Opa were quite animated; they did not applaud either. Mama rushed to the engine room worker and took me off his hands. It is then I noticed some tears in her eyes. I expected to really get it from her because my pretty dress was covered in grease and grime. I must have looked like a little engine room worker, too. Although she scolded me I knew she was not really angry. She made me promise that I would never go down into the engine room again and that I would never take off exploring again on my own, period! I made the required promise, but in my mind it was good only for the rest of the day.

After the engine room drama, I was vigilantly watched nearly round the clock. Mama and Papa had been diplomatically read the "riot act" by the ship's captain to keep tighter reigns on me. My dearest Opa helped keep me amused; he distracted me from my roving ways as much as possible. I was usually on my best behaviour in his company. He played games with me and told me fascinating stories. We would go for nice long walks, a habit we would continue for many years afterwards. Mama often said I had Opa's walking legs. Sometimes I played with other kids on the ship; but I think that most of them had been warned to stay away from me, as if I might get them into trouble, too. No matter, I was quite capable of amusing myself.

In addition to constantly keeping Mama and Papa on edge with my adventurous ways, I was forever embarrassing them. At mealtimes in the large sumptuous dining room, I shamelessly ventured from table to table begging for lumps of sugar and other delicacies. One warm day by the pool, in which Mama and Papa loved frolicking, they decided to introduce me to the joys of swimming. I instantly discovered that I did not like being in a volume of water any larger than a bath and relayed this to them with ear-splitting shrieks of displeasure. This water exercise was soon abandoned and never attempted again. Although Mama and Papa were mortified by my attention-grabbing display in the pool, the other bathers only found it amusing.

Everybody on board already knew of little Hannah, the German girl with the cute Shirley Temple curls, winning smile, and mischievous ways.

Poolside on the Julio César

Still, I continued to be a handful for poor Mama. One day I made my escape and went exploring again. I sauntered onto the bridge because I had been told that the big ship was steered from there. I wanted to see this place for myself. When I entered the wheel-house there indeed was the stern looking captain steering the ship with a large spoked wheel. There were also officers in crisp uniforms. "Hello, Herr Kapitän. It is me, Hannelore Heinemann," I said and dropped him a curtsey. "I would like to see you steer the ship." The captain's eyes rolled towards the bulkhead, and he let out a long, slow breath. I firmly planted my feet to the deck and crossed my arms, not unlike that which he had done that day of my engine room adventure; and I glanced at him with a twinkle in my eye instead of the stern gaze he had given me then. It did the trick and he invited me to stay, but only for a little while. "Show Signorina Heinemann around," he said to one of the officers and then proceeded to ignore me. I was shown around the bridge by the officer and he explained to me the purpose of everything there: these were things that I did not understand and information I forgot right away. It was fascinating, though, especially the colourful maps he referred to as navigation charts. The panoramic view of the deep blue sea totally took me aback. It burned into my brain like a tattoo. Another officer gave me some butter cookies and a glass of milk. I devoured the cookies and gulped down the milk, and escorted back to my cabin. The officer happened to wake Mama, who was taking an afternoon nap. She was dismayed that I had once again managed to sneak away; I was, after all, supposed to be napping as well. Mama made the necessary apologies to the officer while shooting irate glances towards me. "I think this one should have been a boy, Signora. I have never known such an adventurous little girl before," the officer said as he departed. I do not think that Mama considered this a compliment, but I sure did.

Aboard the *Julio César* there was the usual shipboard entertainment for adults, ranging from movies to ballroom dances, playing cards in one of the lounges to shuffleboard on deck. Reading and gossiping while lounging in deck chairs seemed to be another favourite pastime for the grownups. But all activity was conducted in a reserved sort of way because the passengers were sailing into an unknown future. For me, this was the vacation of a lifetime. Mama and Papa enjoyed the social life as much as possible. Opa, however, was still bewildered by what was happening to him and his family. He was, at sixty years of age, much less pliable to dramatic changes in life than his daughter and son-in-law.

At one stage of the trip, Julius Schloss, a musician whom Mama and Papa had befriended, offered to spend time with me in order to give my beleaguered mother a break. I was not too keen on having him babysit me and I hemmed and hawed as he manoeuvred me around the ship. He hit upon the idea of taking me to the bridge. He seemed to believe that this visit would impress me, as he apparently was quite friendly with the captain. Much to the kind-hearted musician's chagrin, the captain informed him that I was well known to him, being a frequent visitor. Herr Schloss did not volunteer his babysitting services much more after his first experience with me.

Musician Julius Schloss on the Julio César

As for me, I did not think I needed a babysitter or anyone else, except Opa maybe, to show me around the ship. I was quite capable of getting around on my own. For the rest of the journey I stayed out of trouble to the best of my ability, much to the delight of Mama. I did provoke one more incident, however, which basically put the icing on the troublesome cake I had been baking since we left Genoa; this took place on the final night aboard ship.

The traditional end-of-journey dinner, which was followed by a dance in the grand ballroom, was interrupted at midnight by the presence of a little girl. She stood stark naked in the doorway, very loudly calling for her Mama. Yes, it was me! With every eye upon her, Mama, with cheeks glowing red, made her way across the room, picked up her embarrassment of a child, and proceeded to our cabin. There she encountered a very unhappy Italian crew member who was my babysitter for the evening, angry and agitated because she had lost her charge. The harried woman was overly apologetic, probably worried she was not going to be paid, but Mama assured her that she was not at fault. The harried babysitter did get paid. On her way out of the cabin she mumbled some words in my direction that did not at all sound complimentary.

Fortunately, at least for everyone who had been affected and stressed by my itinerant behaviour, the journey on the *Julio César* came to an end without any more unfortunate episodes. Those disasters would come later in my new reality: the reality of Shanghai and the mysterious Orient. There, many dramatic incidents would play themselves out all around me as I grew from a precocious three-year-old into a strong-minded, independent teenager.

2

Shanghai 1939 - 1946

A NEW DIMENSION

As the *Julio César* manoeuvred out of the rolling Pacific and into the East China Sea, it set course for our final destination, Shanghai. This legendary "Treaty Port" lies in the delta of the Yangtze River, one of the world's great rivers. At 3,720 miles, it is the longest river in Asia.

The passengers gathered on deck to watch their new home come into view. It was both an awesome and a somewhat disturbing sight. This enormous city that lay sprawled before us, just south of the Yangtze's mouth, was the largest and most industrialised in China. It had a history of more than a thousand years and a population that exceeded three million people, including forty thousand Europeans and Americans. Sailing into the expansive harbour of Shanghai was like sailing into some strange new dimension. My senses were bombarded by an array of stimuli totally alien to me. And even though it was only the middle of May, the weather was very hot and sticky.

The boat made its way through the watery jungle of bizarre Chinese vessels, which included magnificent junks, lowly sampans, water rickshaws, and an assortment of fishing boats. These indigenous craft somehow mingled without incident among freighters and passenger ships of all shapes and sizes, flying flags from countries all over the world.

The blue water of the sea gave way to a brownish–grey soup of the harbour, littered with debris and, what looked like, the bodies of animals or even human beings. As our ship made its way up the Whangpoo River, where the *Julio César* was destined to dock, our nostrils were assaulted by a nauseating cocktail of brackish-smelling harbour water; dead fish; raw sewage; rotting garbage; and thick black smoke, which belched from the stacks of a myriad of steamships. From the shore wafted a haze of industrial pollution, which was compounded by the exhaust fumes from a steady flow of trucks, buses, and automobiles that traversed the busy streets of the waterfront. It seemed as though natural instinct for everyone on board was to throw up; many breathed through handkerchiefs to diffuse the odours.

Our ears were also overwhelmed. They were subjected to blasts from ships' horns, a cacophony of vehicular traffic, the ringing of bicycle bells, as well as the shouts emanating from the swarms of bicyclists, pedicab drivers, and rickshaw coolies. Filtering though this incessant noise was the strange atonal chanting of labourers, distinctive in their triangular straw hats, carrying their heavy loads. What confronted us was the epitome of culture shock.

Once known as an adventurer's paradise and a hotbed for intrigue of all kinds, the Shanghai we were adopting as our new home had evolved into very much a twentieth-century city. With its booming commerce and modern western-style highrise buildings, this ancient city was a key centre of business in Asia that rivalled Hong Kong and Tokyo. Despite the troubled times and Japanese occupation, Shanghai remained a significant hub of intellectual, cultural, and political activity; however, it was a city in transition and on the verge of sacrificing its identity. Shanghai of the late 1930s was a city that had lost a good deal of its former glamour. Some sections still bore the scars from the heavy fighting and bombings perpetrated by the Japanese during the siege of Shanghai in 1937. Although the victorious Japanese did not take over the city proper until December 1941, they used the strategic waterfront district of Hongkew, the poorest section of Shanghai's International Settlement, to house troops and dock warships. The city area that most of the boatloads of Jewish refugees filtered into was this very same Hongkew: a squalid, rat-infested, and overcrowded neighbourhood on the Whangpoo River.

The *Julio César* docked among the blackened ruins of this Japanese stronghold. Our journey was over. While most of the ship's passengers almost reluctantly disembarked with a sense of dread, Mama proclaimed that she felt like she had come home. Because of her avid interest in matters of the paranormal and the occult, she was a firm believer in reincarnation and believed she had spent past lives in China. "We will do well here. I feel it. We have a destiny here," she said to Papa as we made our way off the ship. Papa accepted Mama's philosophical bent without question. He was certain that despite the hardships that were in store for us we would indeed survive here and perhaps even prosper, if that was the correct term to use under the circumstances.

Some of the newcomers were welcomed by relatives who had arrived earlier, but most, including my family, were met by a Jewish relief committee member whose aim was to help process the arrivals.

Shanghai at the time of the arrival of Jewish refugees.
The Soochow Creek flows into the Whangpoo River at the Bund
(Photo courtesy of Ralph Harpuder's Shanghai Memorabilia Collection)

Long before the influx of European Jews to Shanghai, Sephardim Jews from British-ruled areas such as Baghdad, Bombay, and Hong Kong had made their homes in Shanghai since as far back as the mid-1800s. Russian Jews started arriving in Shanghai during the early 1900s, after the pogroms and the Bolshevik Revolution. By the late 1930s, there were over six thousand Russian Jews in Shanghai, outnumbering the approximately one thousand two hundred Sephardim. Many Russian and Sephardim Jews rose from modest to high economic standards; but of the two existing communities, the Sephardim became the most prosperous group and dominated Jewish life in Shanghai.

By the time of our arrival, when it was clear that the number of new arrivals would be quite significant, a few very wealthy Middle Eastern Jewish families felt it their philanthropic duty to assist the nearly penniless refugees. It was the well-known Sephardim families such as the Sassoons, Kadoories, and Hardouns who organized or funded schools and kindergartens, soup kitchens, and other relief measures for the new immigrants. Until the United States entered into WWII on December 8, 1941, the day after the bombing of Pearl Harbor, a great deal of support came from American Jewish groups as well. This humanitarian effort was spearheaded in Shanghai by an angel of mercy by the name of Laura Margolis, who was personally credited with saving the lives of some four thousand Jews.

The first and foremost concern of the refuge committees was to find homes for the new arrivals. Because rooms were difficult to obtain and were at a premium, refugee camps called "Heime" were established. These consisted of hastily converted warehouses and storage facilities. Large rooms were assigned to families or a number of individuals. The only source of privacy was a flimsy curtain or blanket that separated the two- or three-decker bunk beds from those of their neighbours. The majority of refugees did not have the means to consider alternatives to the Heime and, and as a result, were taken there by trucks after disembarking and were processed as refugees.

The adjustment from what was a comfortable middle-class existence in Germany and Austria to these new horrific living arrangements in the Heime came as a great shock to those who were subjected to them. Yet, somehow, the human ability to adjust to the most extreme situations made it possible for most to survive. Unfortunately, the abysmal times that were thrust upon us would get much worse before they got better.

Because my family had managed to bring some goods of value and negotiable currency out of Germany, we were among the more fortunate newcomers to Shanghai and were able to avoid the refugee camps. Through the relief committee, we obtained a single ground-floor room in a dilapidated private house. Although this was considerably better than the chaos and overcrowding of the Heime, it was hardly the lap of luxury. For Mama, Papa, and Opa, who had lived their entire lives in comfortable surroundings, this was just a level above rock bottom. The room was located in one of a series of row houses near the unpleasant docks of the Whangpoo River. Living conditions here were primitive. There were no sewers in Hongkew and raw sewage abounded; the filthy odour somehow blended with the much more bearable scents of charcoal fires, boiling soup, roasted meat, and sweet jasmine. The area teemed with vermin of all kinds. It was a fulltime job to keep ahead of them.

Shortly after our arrival, a large rat visited me one night; the creature seemed friendly enough and I played with it as if it were a house pet. Having never seen a rat, I did not recognize this animal and mistook it for something much more benign. When I told Mama the next day that a nice squirrel had come to play with me, I could tell by the horror in her eyes that my new friend was no friend. "Never touch one of those vile creatures again, Hannelore. You may get bitten and they can make you sick," she warned me. Right away she changed my bedding in case the rat has deposited lice or other parasites. She then convened a council of war against the unwanted guests with the acquisition of a fierce cat. We called him Heika, and even though he was a proficient rat-killing machine, to my delight I was allowed to play with him. Heika took a shine to me and at once I made him my personal pet. He would prove to be a real survivor and remained with us for many years to come.

Hannelore and Heika, 1939

The endemic rat situation also led to a new career for Opa: that of exterminator. The once successful haberdasher apprenticed with a professional exterminator who, like most of the people we met, was a fellow immigrant. He had, however, been in Shanghai for many years as part of a small German community, a community that was gradually becoming the largest European ethnic group in the city. The two of them were kept quite busy in a never-ending feud with the vermin for control of Hongkew. Papa, meanwhile, could not immediately pursue his chosen career as a bookseller. But as he was not above menial tasks, he earned a few pennies helping new arrivals unload their baggage from the ships.

And so we settled into our new lives. I was enrolled into the kindergarten of one of the schools funded by the Kadoories which was staffed by some of their family members. Everyone, it seemed, pitched in to contribute some kind of service. One such lady very generously took home children to spend the night with her and her family. This was considered the ultimate treat and honour: one glorious night spent away from the dire conditions of Hongkew. She provided a hot bath, new clothes, and a wonderful meal in her luxurious home. I did not give this altruistic behaviour much thought because as a three-year-old adventurer, I did not have a problem with Hongkew. For me it was just some strange setting, which was at the opposite end of the scale from where I had lived in Berlin.

When it was finally my turn to spend the night with this wonderful lady, her act of kindness seemed more like some kind of abduction. I felt very ill at ease and just wanted to be home with Mama. I did not care about the bath, as being immersed in water was not exactly one of my favourite pastimes; and nobody was a better cook than my own mother. Even the new clothes failed to placate me because I was not short of pretty things to wear. Mama was an accomplished seamstress and made sure I was always very nicely dressed.

In fact, nothing the lady did comforted me. Eventually, my hollering and screeching drove my poor hostess to take me home in the middle of the night. Heavy rain was pouring from the dark skies when she hailed a taxi and escorted me back to the slums of Hongkew. We woke Mama and Papa, who came befuddled to the door in their nightclothes. They were surprised to see me rush past them into the room, leaving it to my benefactor to explain why we had roused them from their sleep. Needless to say, this episode consumed Mama with embarrassment. But then, she was no stranger to being embarrassed by me and knew her Hannelore was very much Mama's little girl. We had been inseparable since my birth. The only time we were not together was when I was at school or taking off on one of my adventures, which was the only time I did not seem to need her.

There was so much to explore in Hongkew, and I had a new task at hand, that of learning English. All lessons were taught in the King's English, which I assumed was to better prepare us for life in the city. I thought I would need to learn Chinese, but it turned out that English was the necessary language for getting around. In Shanghai, I continued to be the fearless explorer I had become aboard the *Julio César*, and people all over the district reported seeing me on my outings. My family would only live in Hongkew for about nine months, but during that time some of my exploits became the stuff of legend–at least in my own mind. I did my best to live up to my reputation.

I also took it upon myself to socialize with the grownups of the community, minus the company of Mama and Papa. One such occasion came to Mama's attention in the most roundabout fashion, further proof that I was the talk of the town and that nothing escaped her. A lady in the neighbourhood, whom Mama had befriended, came to her one day with the latest report of my activities. "I was in the beauty parlour today and overheard a most interesting conversation between two women that I had never seen before," Mama's friend told her. "One of the ladies was describing a party she had given to celebrate her birthday. An invited couple arrived, accompanied by a pretty young girl. The couple thought the child was a neighbour and that she had been invited. The hostess thought the child had come with the couple. For a while all went well. Cake and cocoa were served, something the uninvited young guest was more than happy to partake in. The girl relentlessly chatted up everybody until one of the guests asked her name, upon which the intruder blurted out: 'Hannelore Heinemann.' Then, the girl promptly vanished." I was glad to be at school when our tattletale neighbour told Mama about my escapade. Luckily, by the time I got home, Mama had come to see the humour in it.

Mama was constantly worried about me, and it took her a while to realize that I was perfectly safe in Hongkew. No Chinese person would dare harm a little white child. There was friendly curiosity because of my blond curls;

quite often the Chinese women, who were usually reserved, came up to me to touch my hair and see if it was real. I let them touch it, pleased to be such a centre of attraction. Sometimes it elicited a giggle from them or a comment that I assumed was complimentary. After I had let them fuss over me for a few moments I took off like a whirlwind, just in case they decided to cut off a strand to take home as a souvenir.

I was not yet fully aware why we traded our beautiful home and the immaculately clean and orderly streets of Berlin for our shabby new residence and the filth and chaos of Hongkew, but to me it did not matter, as this place was much more interesting. The streets were a constant ebb and flow of activities as more and more refugees made their way into the city. I liked to mingle with the street people, that is, whenever I could sneak off from our room by the docks. There seemed to be as many Caucasian people selling their wares as there were Chinese. It was like some kind of never-ending bazaar or flea market. I did not realize that the white people were desperate fellow Jews selling their belongings to make ends meet. Most of them could find no work and eventually, when they ran out of things to sell, they were penniless. The daily trials and tribulations of their difficult existence escaped me, and I was under the impression that everyone had gathered here for a life of adventure.

In addition to my outrageous antics, I became known around Hongkew for another reason, that of a pint-sized entertainer. It was one of the things Mama really could take pride in. With the influx of refugees, a new social life was establishing itself. This one saw the opening of all kinds of small businesses including European coffee houses, restaurants, bars, and theatres. Musicians, performers, and former entertainers had the opportunity to once again pursue their livelihoods. Mama and Papa, and sometimes Opa, enjoyed Sunday afternoon gatherings in the coffee houses. From time to time, I was encouraged to do a little song and dance, performing popular tunes of the day. Mama, of course, always made sure I was suitably dressed for these occasions. She could turn the simplest and most modest of fabrics into clothing that would not have been out of place in a fashionable department store. I think that maybe she liked showing me off in her wonderful couture creations. But that was okay; I liked to show off in them.

I was hardly a talent of revelation by any means, but my winning smile more than made up for it in the eyes of the audience. Actually, I was quite a hit among Mama and Papa's new friends and the clientele of the coffee houses. They were very proud of me and it pleased me to please them. I suppose this made up for all my non-sanctioned adventures and mischief. I learned later that my paternal grandmother, Lotte Gumpel, had been a vaudeville and theatre actress back in Germany. Perhaps that explained my desire to perform in front of an audience and ham it up. Like most child performers, however, my entertainment career was short lived; not that I aspired to be an actress or singer.

Our family had nicely settled into our refugee lives, but the enervating heat-filled summer months were especially difficult for Mama. She would never acclimatize to the weather despite all the years we would spend in Shanghai. Papa, meanwhile, was very busy re-establishing himself as an antiquarian bookseller. Within three months of our arrival in Shanghai, he had been able to cease working as a humble baggage handler. He assiduously networked and made business connections to facilitate his ability to work once again in his chosen field. He bought and sold books all over town and started harbouring the thought of opening up his own bookshop again, although it would take a bit more time to turn it into an actuality.

That summer we experienced our first typhoon. Coming from a city with relatively sedate weather like Berlin, the magnitude of these storms was very frightening to us. Huge volumes of water were dumped on the city, which, in combination with wind swept tides, caused severe flooding.

When the annual typhoon season struck Shanghai, usually between July and September, the Whangpoo River overflowed and streets disappeared under brackish water up to three feet deep. This filthy water seeped everywhere and was a breeding ground for the many enteric type diseases that were so prevalent in Shanghai. In Hongkew, the already physically weakened refugees were easy targets. Although Hongkew was particularly vulnerable because of its close proximity to the Whangpoo River, the typhoons respected no boundaries. They caused misery and devastation in all three municipal districts: the International Settlement, the French Concession, and Greater Shanghai.

Typhoon season in Shanghai
(Photo courtesy of Ralph Harpuder's Shanghai Memorabilia Collection)

As 1939 approached 1940, living conditions became even more uncomfortable and crowded in Hongkew. A severe attack of amoebic dysentery affected our family, of which Mama and I were its chief targets. I was so sick that my family feared for my life. Their little explorer was grounded in a most debilitating way. There was no medical help available. So, Mama, despite being very ill, used home remedies as well as her medical knowledge to nurse me day and night from the brink of death. It became critical, however, that in order for me to recuperate totally, we would have to leave the unhealthy surroundings of the Hongkew docks. There was illness all around us and many people died. Papa had already been thinking of moving us out of the slum, but the illness that had struck his wife and child prompted him to seek new living accommodations in earnest. Although I completely got over the illness, Mama was not as fortunate: for the rest of her life she would be afflicted by intestinal problems.

By late December 1939, we felt well enough to celebrate our first Christmas in Shanghai. Despite being a Jewish family, we recognized this Christian holiday because of Papa's Lutheran upbringing. Even Opa, as a devout Jew, joined in the festivities. We had many things to celebrate: our escape from Germany, safe voyage to Shanghai, the improving health of Mama and myself, and the prospect of moving to a new home.

樂安麗娜 THE FRENCH CONCESSION

Shortly into the New Year, Papa found a modern apartment at the other end of the city, in the fabled French Concession. This area was about as far away from Hongkew as one could get, literally and figuratively. The French Concession, located in southwest Shanghai, was the upscale area of the International Settlement. The original Concession had been comprised of a mere 164 acres but underwent various increases in scope until it escalated to 2,525 acres, slightly less than half of the entire International Settlement.

We gathered our few possessions including a large oak table that had come with us from Berlin, and made our exit from Hongkew in early February 1940. Although the move to the French Concession meant very little to me, once there, I was delighted by my new surroundings. In stark contrast to the slums of Hongkew, the streets in the French Concession were wide and clean and planted with leafy trees. Life was not as frenetic here and the air was much cleaner. There were impressive Art Deco buildings, splendid western-style mansions, and beautifully groomed gardens. The Concession was a hub of trendy shops, cabaret clubs, and lively theatres. It was so French that it had been dubbed the "Paris of the Orient." Many years later when I actually visited Paris, I thought it looked just like Shanghai.

Although the French Concession was all glamour on the outside, it had an underbelly of lawlessness and decadence. It was a hotbed for organized crime and much of its municipal revenue was raised from the licensing of opium dens, brothels, and gambling houses. These, as well as all other criminal activities, were either directly controlled by the notorious Triads or were under their influence by means of extortion. Shanghai was to the Triads what Palermo, Sicily, was to La Cosa Nostra. The Triads, however, coexisted nicely with the French authorities and the politicos of the International Settlement. In fact, the Triads were cosy with everybody, from the police and ruling Nationalist Party to the Communists and the Japanese occupying forces. Whatever was good for business was good for the Triads.

I was not concerned with the notoriety of the French Concession, however. For me it was a brand new territory of exploration and adventure. The time I spent in this environment was among the happiest of my Shanghai interlude. Our home in the newly developing suburb of Prosper Paris was at the end of a long row of recently built attached houses. Each apartment unit contained two bedrooms, a dining-living room, a kitchen, and a bathroom. We were on the ground floor and had a lovely little veranda where we could sit outside and where we took meals when the weather permitted. This apartment was quite palatial compared to our previous home in Hongkew, and Papa and Mama had to acquire additional furniture to fill it. We all loved our new home. Mama, Papa, and Opa were once again living in surroundings to which they were a little more accustomed.

As in Hongkew, I was happiest outdoors. I explored brand new territory, marvelled at the wonderful homes, the luscious gardens, the fancy stores, and the energetic cafés. I believed that the gardens had been put there especially for me. Compared to my former stomping grounds, this place was paradise. When the multifarious flowering plants and trees were in bloom, the air was sweet and fragrant compared to Hongkew. My favourite playing ground was a large empty lot directly behind our apartment. It was covered with weeds and pretty wildflowers. The focal point, however, was the remains of an ancient house, which I at once imagined to be a castle destroyed by a fierce dragon. I spent many hours playing there and, when the mood struck me, I picked some of the wildflowers to take home to Mama.

Not long after moving to Prosper Paris I befriended a little boy whose father owned a wafer factory. Every now and then we would go to the factory and were presented with a brown paper bag containing bits and pieces of the delicious wafers baked there. It really did not get any better than this. I also spent much more time with my loving Opa. He became my near constant companion and best friend. Since moving to our new home he had become more and more centred in his religion. Opa was the most devout of Jews and was very community minded, giving as much of himself for the betterment of others as he could.

Living miles away from Hongkew, I could no longer attend the Kadoorie School, so new day care arrangements were made for me. News that a member of the British community had opened such a facility called Peter Pan School reached Mama and Papa, and I was promptly enrolled. The lady in charge was a "stiff upper-lip" type and ran the establishment quite strictly, somewhat like a junior army boot camp. She soon came face to face with the young rebellious and independent person I had become. As a result, I provided a daily challenge to her attempts to curb her unruly charge. Despite having her hands full with me, I knew she took a liking to me. Even when she felt the need to scold me, she sometimes had to work hard at not letting her bemusement show through. My golden locks and disarming smile did it every time.

At home we always spoke German, but I was becoming more fluent in English everyday. And because I spent so much time on the streets, I picked up enough Chinese to converse on a basic level. Mama was a little less worried about my safety in our new surroundings; the French Concession was a swanky neighbourhood after all. She had some concerns, however, about the drug-addicted beggars who drifted in and out of the opium dens and who lingered on the streets just long enough to secure a few pennies for their next fix. "I want you to stay away from those poor wretched creatures because they don't know what they're doing," Mama cautioned me. She told me that their minds and bodies had been poisoned.

Still, I was safe enough around the denizens of the French Concession, but that did not always mean that I was safe around myself. While playing in the street one day, I absentmindedly ran into a streetcar that was continuing on its way after having made a scheduled stop. The horrified conductor and some of the passengers piled out of the vehicle to see if I was all right. Although this incident could have caused serious injuries, I survived with just a few scrapes and bruises and a minor cut to my forehead. I did not even shed a tear as I picked myself up off the street. Using a mish-mash of German, broken English, and even more broken Chinese, I assured the concerned conductor, passengers, and curious onlookers that I was okay. The conductor and passengers, satisfied that I was indeed no worse for the experience, re-boarded the streetcar and continued on their way; however, a group of inquisitive Chinese pedestrians followed me home. For some reason they did this at a respectful distance. They were, I would assume, totally mystified by the little white girl who had clashed with a Shanghai streetcar and survived.

When we got to Prosper Paris, Mama, who happened to be outside hanging up some clothes, saw the apparition of her child, covered in blood and followed by a crowd. As I approached her, I noticed that she was even more horrified than the conductor had been. I thought I was going to be in big trouble. "Hannelore! My God! What happened to you?" she shrieked. Mama scanned the faces of my Chinese entourage, as if for a clue. All she got was a collection of polite bows, nods, grins, smiles, and wild gestures. Convinced she was not going to learn anything from this group, Mama picked me up and hurried me into the house. "Honestly, Hannelore, you'll be the death of me. Why can't you behave like other little girls and just play with your toys?" she admonished. I reminded her that I did play with my dolly Lisa and lion Zoltar, and even with Heika the supercat. She put me in the dreaded bath to wash off the caked-on blood and gave me a thorough examination. As it turned out, the blood had come from just a small cut to the head which was easily covered by a plaster. Mama demanded again to know what had happened. While she put me into clean clothes, I finally explained about my mishap with the streetcar.

Mama was alarmed, not just by the prospect of what could have been a serious injury, but also by the legal implications. She assumed that the streetcar driver had recorded the accident in his daily logbook and there was a need to bring official closure. We hastily proceeded to the nearest police station to report the incident. The police officials were quite friendly and showed great concern, asking Mama if perhaps I should not be taken to the hospital for an examination. She told them of her medical background, that she had examined me herself, and that I would be just fine. A report was written up by one of the policemen and was signed by my mother. That was the end of it, much to my relief because I was afraid I might get thrown in jail. "I hope you have learned a lesson from all this," Mama said to me on the way home. I assured her I had, although I was not quite clear on what it was I had learned.

After the streetcar incident, Mama tried to keep me on a short leash as much as possible. As usual, after getting into major trouble I limited my activities to more low-key affairs for the next few days, such as playing with Heika and my toys and reading books that Papa brought home for me.

One of the new connections Papa had made on his book buying and selling rounds was a very likeable Austrian named Kurt Schwartz. Mr. Schwartz was a dashing adventurer type who had been drawn to Shanghai in the early 1930s, like so many other young men looking for action and opportunity in an "open city." Papa took a liking to him at once, not so much because of Mr. Schwartz's bent for excitement but because he was also an avid student of literature and the fine arts. Meeting Mr. Schwartz proved to be auspicious for Papa because they entered into a partnership that led Papa to open a bookshop in the French Concession. This partnership, in addition to its business value, provided Papa with the assurance that he did not have to worry about restrictions in his movements, something that affected all stateless persons more and more as time ebbed away, even in wide-open Shanghai.

Papa inside the Western Arts Gallery, Avenue Joffre, Shanghai

Papa and Mr. Schwartz opened the bookshop in a retail space shared with Mr. Tsao, whose store specialized in fine art objects and rare Chinese curios. The store, which was located in the elegant Henry Mansions on Avenue Joffre, was in one of the most prestigious shopping areas in the Concession and was an excellent location to launch such a venture. The bookstore was a perfect complement to Mr. Tsao's inventory. The shop, which the new partners called the Western Arts Gallery, proved to be an instant success. This success was not really surprising to us, as Papa, who took care of the day-to-day activities of the store, had the highest expectations of himself and was most assiduous in everything he did. His expertise covered all areas of books, from the mundane to the most rare and precious. Like he had done in Berlin, he catered to the reading tastes of a large, cosmopolitan, well-educated public. Among his customers were bookish Europeans, especially members of the diplomatic core. Soon, the clientele grew to include Chinese, Japanese, and Russian patrons: a veritable cross-section of the population of Shanghai.

Papa's undeniable charm and knack for telling engaging stories endeared him to young and old, male and female. One of his better known clients was Lothar Brieger, a renowned German literary critic who was also one of the more fortunate Jews to have escaped his homeland after the Nazi takeover. On their daily walks, Mr. Brieger and his cute little dog, Biche, would drop by the bookstore. Scholarly discussions abounded between Papa, Mr. Brieger, and the other regulars. The Western Arts Gallery was so successful that Papa needed help with correspondence, cataloguing, and sales. He hired Illo

Koratkowski, his own "Girl Friday." Illo was the daughter of Papa's accountant, Paul Koratkowski, a fellow refugee from Berlin. Mr. Koratkowski had been the managing director of a Berlin bank in better times and was very astute with figures and money matters. Illo was a pretty eighteen-year-old girl. What she lacked in practical work experience, she made up with her enthusiasm for learning the rare books business. Illo and her fiancé, Ernest Heppner, became close friends of Mama and Papa. Ernest later became one of the first writers to document the Jewish experience in Shanghai in a book entitled *Shanghai Refuge-A Memoir of the World War II Jewish Ghetto.* Illo remained in Papa's employ for a number of years and would turn out to be the best and most dedicated of all those who worked at the bookshop.

Unidentified, Mr. Tsao, Illo Koratkowski Heppner, and Papa at the Western Arts Gallery, Avenue Joffre, Shanghai

Although the Western Arts Gallery was quite a distance from Prosper Paris, it became one of my favourite destinations. I often nagged Mama or Opa to take me there. It was always a treat when one, or both, took me for a visit. What captured my imagination the most was Mr. Tsao's half of the store. At first, the venerable old gentleman was a bit concerned about the rambunctious little Heinemann kid, but, like everybody else, he fell under my spell and we became buddies. Mr. Tsao was one of the few Chinese people I got to know personally during my early years in Shanghai. He was a wonderful man, well-educated, and held in high esteem in the world of rare Chinese artefacts. Mr. Tsao appreciated my keen interest in his goods and taught me about the many treasures in the shop. I think that in addition to teaching me a little about the history and rarity of these objects, he liked to hint at their value so I would not go tear-housing around, which I did not dream of doing. Papa, in his most serious of fatherly looks, had already laid down the law for me. "You are to do what Mr. Tsao tells you and behave like a perfect little lady when you are in the store," he cautioned me. And here I thought I was a perfect little lady at all times! During most of my visits there, however, I preferred to play outside. Located at the back of the apartment complex that housed the store was a beautiful park. I loved to frolic on the manicured lawns and smell the lovely flowers.

After living in Shanghai for a number of years, I came to realize that there were several distinct layers to this intriguing city. These were layers with surprisingly little overlap between them. It seemed that most foreigners in this most international city had minimal contact with the indigenous Chinese population around them. Fewer still bothered to learn basic Chinese.

Considering that most Chinese in Shanghai were denied the comforts and privileges enjoyed by their western guests, life for the average Chinese citizen in this city was better than in most other areas of their country. Under the system of a limited government influenced by the foreign-controlled enclave, low taxes, and economic laissez faire, Shanghai was by far the most prosperous metropolis in all of Asia. The standard of living of Chinese residents in the International Settlement and in the surrounding Chinese-administered areas was the highest in East Asia.

Inevitably, many of the 800,000 Chinese who lived in the Settlement and Concession took a fancy to the slick western culture that had integrated itself in the city. Inevitably, they adopted foreign-influenced habits, dress, and speech. The Settlement was a veritable cauldron of cultures, where East met West and galvanized the two into a melding of identities. This was my Shanghai, a Shanghai I slowly came to discover and love; one that continuously kept me in awe. Perhaps I shared Mama's affinity for the place because I, too, believed that I had been here before in some other life.

Following our move to the French Concession in early 1940, life for the Heinemanns and Opa Silberstein was good for the next two years and we prospered. And, in the naiveté of childhood, I assumed that everyone else moved along in life and did well, too. Later I came to understand that we prospered because of Papa's resourcefulness and ability to turn liabilities into assets. Papa was a strong-minded person with a very positive life philosophy: he simply refused to accept adverse situations. Papa knew that while luck was a key element in succeeding, one needed to be an active participant. "You have to be a driver and not just a passenger along for the ride if success is to be achieved and sustained," he was fond of saying. He worked countless hours and was very diligent in all his affairs. Since the opening of the Western Arts Gallery, Papa was in his element again, selling books and searching out rare editions for discerning clients. If Papa could not get the book then more than likely it was not available in China.

Opa, however, had more or less come to terms with his new life but still missed Berlin and, most of all, his dear deceased wife Helene. He would always miss her, as he would his Berlin.

Mama, unfortunately, did not pursue her profession of dentistry. She considered the possibilities, but the difficulty and expense of setting up a practice were discouraging. Most professionals shared offices, which were hard to find. They also had to stagger their working hours in order to accommodate one another. This work situation did not appeal to Mama. The bout of illness that had afflicted her in Hongkew had weakened her; problems with her health were always at hand during extreme weather conditions. Thus, she had decided that her place was at home looking after her family and trying to stay healthy. "I love Shanghai; I love the people, but the climate they can keep," Mama would often say whenever she was not feeling well.

In 1940, I was almost five years old and loving life which was a daily routine of exploration, adventure, and school. The latter I did not love as much as the former.

Long walks with Opa had become one of the highlights of my day. He particularly liked walking in the nearby countryside.

On rare occasions, Opa and I went to a matinee performance at a small local theatre and watched an American movie. Laurel and Hardy were my absolute favourites. Opa, however, was not a big fan of movies. Watching American movies helped me with my English, although it sounded different from the King's English, which was the version taught in Shanghai. To Opa, the English language may as well have been Greek: it all sounded foreign to him. "What is so funny? What did they just say?" he would ask in German whenever the theatre erupted in laughter, and I would try the best I could to translate. But the physical antics of Laurel and Hardy needed no interpretation, and Opa roared with me and the rest of the audience. Opa and I also regularly passed many a pleasant hour on the veranda of our apartment. He recounted amusing tales or shared his wisdom with me. Much of what he imparted to me regarded our ancestry and Judaism. I did not quite understand most of these things, but he told me not to worry because someday I would.

While we made a new life for ourselves in Prosper Paris during the course of 1940, the menace we had left behind in Germany had spread over much of Europe. An event that sent shivers through Shanghai's Jewish community took place on September 27, 1940. Japan signed the Tripartite Pact with Germany and Italy, thus forming the infamous Axis. The possible consequence of the pact haunted the minds of not only the refugee community but the established Sephardim and White Russians, as well.

Everyone wondered if the safe haven of Shanghai, which now had the largest Jewish community in the Far East, would remain as such.

猶太避難民調查表
DIRECTORY OF JEWISH REFUGEES

番號 No. 2831

30 MAR. 1940

本件差支無之
右許可ス

姓名 Name in full	Heinz-Egon Israel H e i n e m a n n
男女別 Sex	male
年齢 Age	27 years
國籍 Nationality	German
使用言語 Language	German, English
現住所 Address	Shanghai, Broadway East 1166 /32. Room 3.
職業又ハ特技 Occupation or Ability	Art-and bookseller.-Art-expert.
教育程度 Education	Classical school of the first grade. College.
宗教 Religion	XXXXXX. Protestant.
資産 Means	Moderate.

旅券番號 Passport No.	發給官廳 Issued by	日時 On
II/6750/38	Berlin Police	21. Dec. 1938.

Directory of Jewish Refugees, March 30, 1940

The troublesome incidents that took place locally and in Europe were whispered about in my presence or talked about behind my back. Mama, Papa, and Opa had no intention of troubling me with the horrors of the adult world. They did everything possible to ensure I enjoyed a normal, untroubled life; the kind of life that should be the birthright of any child but unfortunately was not to be the case for too many. I was truly privileged in an unprivileged situation. My biggest concern at the time remained getting through the tedium of the day at school.

On the world stage, things moved at a quick pace from bad to worse. In 1941, Yugoslavia and Greece succumbed to Germany, which, shortly thereafter, attacked the Soviet Union despite a non-aggression pact. Japan was not idle during the intervening years either. It conquered French Indo-China, attacked the Dutch East Indies, bombed the U.S. fleet at Pearl Harbor, and attacked the British fleet in the Gulf of Siam. The United States and Britain declared war on Japan on December 8, 1941. A few days later, Germany declared war on the U.S.A. The world had gone totally mad and everyone speculated about what could be in store for Shanghai. Storm clouds were gathering and threatening our seemingly assured future. The attack on Pearl Harbor brought about the complete takeover of Shanghai by Japanese forces. Once again, the world was about to face some drastic changes. An estimated twenty-eight thousand Jews now lived in Shanghai, ranging from the wealthy Sephardim families in their opulent homes to the destitute refugees in the slums of Hongkew. In late 1941, Jews from Lithuania and Poland, were among the last to arrive in Hongkew. The place was truly bursting at the seams.

The worst was yet to come, however. Although the International Settlement, along with the rest of Greater Shanghai, was now under complete Japanese command, the Japanese showed very little interest in the French Concession. France was under Vichy control and deemed an ally of the occupying German forces. The French of Shanghai were not considered to be a threat to the Japanese regime. One of the consequences of total Japanese occupation was the eventual evacuation of most anti-Axis nationals including the British, American, and allied populations. They were interned in prisoner of war camps located on the outskirts of the city.

One afternoon, Opa and I witnessed some of this evacuation as we returned home from one of our daily walks. It was a disturbing sight. We stood at the side of the road with a crowd of Chinese and observed a long convoy of open trucks and lorries that transported men, women, and children to the camps. They would be forced to remain in the camps for the rest of the war. Their horrors would remain secret until the American liberation. In eerie silence we watched what looked like a slow-motion scene in a movie. The people on the trucks were jammed together, their faces masked in fear. Opa clutched my hand more tightly than usual. He understood that what was happening might well be a prelude of what could await us. In fact, the Japanese authorities, who dealt with the Jewish population according to their origin, were already rounding up some Jews. Jews with British documents were, like the British themselves, deemed enemies of the state and interned. Their Shanghai-born relatives or those with passports from other non-enemy countries were not affected.

For the longstanding Sephardic community, the next three-and-a-half years would become part of the collective nightmare. They now understood that even they were not safe in a city they assumed would never threaten them with harm. Families were torn apart and a continuing state of anxiety blanketed the community. Russian Ashkenazi Jews, mainly living in the French Concession, were spared the roundup despite Germany's aggression in Russia. Japan was not at war with the USSR and had no desire to trigger hostilities to its north. The Russo-Japanese border clashes of 1938 in Manchuria were still fresh in the minds of the Japanese so they focused their hostilities in the Pacific.

RETURN TO HONGKEW

In late 1942, Colonel Josef Meisinger, the Gestapo chief for the Far East, proposed to the Japanese government that the "Final Solution" be implemented in Shanghai. This was the diabolical plan for Jewish extermination, drafted at the Wannsee Conference earlier that year in Berlin. Meisinger, known as "The Butcher of Warsaw," had a hard time convincing the Japanese to adopt the Nazi's heinous scheme. Shanghai's Japanese Vice-Consul Mitsugi Shibata was especially indifferent to Meisinger's plan. Shibata was a man of honour and subscribed to the ancient Samurai adage that even a hunter did not kill a bird that flew to him for refuge. He liaised with Jewish leaders to warn them of impending trouble. This move proved to be his undoing, and he was recalled to Tokyo in disgrace for sympathizing with the Jewish community.

Ultimately, the Japanese rejected the Nazi's demands to exterminate the refugees. The Japanese, as well as the Chinese, did not identify with the Aryan concept of anti-Semitism. Except for those holding British or American passports, the Japanese did not perceive the Jews as enemies. Furthermore, the Japanese failed to understand the Germans' obsession with destroying these people, especially the very young and the elderly, who in Asian culture were revered. Still, there was some show of solidarity and, in order to not offend their allies any further, the Japanese authorities arrested and beat Jewish leaders who supposedly "conspired" with Shibata.

To further appease the Nazi's insistence that something be done about the "Jewish Problem," the Japanese created a Jewish community in Hongkew. Against the wishes of their German Axis partners, the Japanese very carefully avoided calling the area a Jewish ghetto and officially labeled it as a restricted area. Despite the euphemism, life for the Shanghai refugees would soon become even more trying.

Then in February 1943, when I was turning seven years old, the Japanese issued a proclamation ordering all stateless European refugees to move into the restricted area of Hongkew. This resettlement had to be carried out by May 18. It was the Japanese answer to the Nazi's Jewish problem. All Jews who arrived in Shanghai after 1937 were affected. By any other name, Hongkew was indeed a ghetto. It was less than one square mile in area and was at that time one of the most densely populated cosmopolitan areas in the world.

Hongkew differed, however, from its infamous European ghetto counterparts in that it was not segregated; it was home to nearly eighty thousand Chinese, thousands of East Indians, and even Japanese civilians. In many ways the fact that segregation was not implemented made the survival of the refugees somewhat easier. The European Jews, who eventually made up close to one quarter of the population of Hongkew, were at liberty to go about their lives and mingle freely with the rest of the residents, as long as they did so within the confines of the ghetto.

Jewish residents needed special passes to venture beyond the carefully monitored boundaries.

Because the possibility of finding accommodations in Hongkew lessened each day, our family returned to the crowded district well before the May relocation deadline. This time there was no knowing when we might be able to leave again. After our charmed lives in the French Concession, the misery of Hongkew was all the more overwhelming. For me it was just another move back to a different environment, albeit a much more unpleasant one.

Papa did his utmost to keep us from having to move into one of the large Heime, which had grown to five in number since 1939. By great good fortune he was able to obtain a room in a rather old, hastily converted house on Alcock Road. The room was located on the ground floor and came with a very small concrete-walled kitchen, which had a single cold-water faucet. As in our previous two Shanghai residences, we found ourselves in a row house at the end of a laneway. "We need to look at this as a good omen. I'm sure we'll be safe here," Mama observed about this rather odd coincidence. Papa nodded his head in silent agreement.

Alcock Road had a number of laneways, as well as one of the larger Heime in close proximity. At one end of the road was a ten-foot-high stone wall topped with pieces of jagged glass. It was part of the enclosure that surrounded the infamous Ward Road Jail. This jail, one of the largest in the Far East, was the disreputable place of torture and temporary imprisonment of those unfortunate enough to run afoul of Japanese rules. Those suspected of committing activities considered dangerous or who contravened wartime laws were interned in this ghastly place. Its vermin and lice-ridden cells, rough treatment, routine daily torture, and lack of medical attention, guaranteed an inevitable death for many inmates. Once a prisoner had passed on, relatives were called to collect the broken and diseased bodies of their loved ones for burial.

The houses of the Alcock Road laneways were quite dilapidated and had been repaired at minimum expense, the quality of work not being a high priority. These pitiable renovations had been hastily carried out in order to rent to the new arrivals. The owners of these buildings were either wealthy Chinese families or foreigners who had invested in the properties some years earlier. It had become quite profitable to rent to desperate refugees. Our new living space measured no more than 15 by 20 feet. It was a shoebox compared to our apartment in Prosper Paris. Papa and Mama were forced, for the second time in their lives, to dispose of most of their belongings. When considering the conditions of the Heime, the dwelling on Alcock Road was nothing short of a palace, and Mama did her best to make it a cosy home.

Opa, Mama, Hannelore, and Papa, Alcock Road, Shanghai

The room was furnished with four beds, which were surprisingly comfortable. My bed was located in a little alcove. It became my own private little refuge after Mama made a curtain to separate it from the beds of the adults. Our large oak table occupied the centre of the room. Its four chairs rested on top of the table to provide a bit more manoeuvrability whenever they were not needed. When I could not play outside, I turned the space underneath the table into my own special little place by hanging blankets over the sides. I spent hours on end amusing myself there with Heika, Lisa, Zoltar, or my other toys.

A coal-fed potbelly stove dominated one end of the room. In order to heat our cramped quarters during the winter months, the potbelly had to be fed a daily quota of coal briquettes. Because coal was difficult to obtain and very expensive, Opa manufactured briquettes by hand out of coal dust. He set up a little production area on the second floor common balcony, patiently adding a bit of water at a time to the dust and forming the mixture into little fuel cakes. Once Opa had performed this messy task, he spread the formations out on newspapers to dry and solidify. This substandard coal was not exactly the most efficient method of sustaining a fire, but the dust was the only form of fuel we could afford. Quite often the result of burning the briquettes was a smoke-filled room. Even on the coldest days, the doors and windows had to be opened until the haze dissipated.

At the opposite end of the room was a door that led out into a tiny wall-enclosed courtyard. It was a poor substitute for the garden I had left behind in the French Concession, but it was better than nothing. I made plans to put in some flowers, but this project never materialized because seeds and flower bulbs were not easily available in Hongkew. A massive wooden door, kept shut at all times, separated this postage stamp of a garden space from the hustle and bustle of the laneway.

Like many other Hongkew accommodations, our dwelling lacked the most basic bathroom facilities. Gone was the flush toilet we enjoyed and took for granted in Prosper Paris: instead we had a primitive bucket-and-seat arrangement, which was communal among the tenants of the house and had to be emptied daily. I was strictly forbidden to make use of this facility and was given a little potty instead.

Very early each morning, the neighbourhood was aroused by a lingering and distinctive odour and a loud voice announcing the arrival of the "Honey Cart," which was a large wooden barrel on wheels. This contraption was pulled by hand and meant to stop at every house to collect and empty the buckets. It was a well-known fact that the contents of these carts were taken to the surrounding farms to be used as fertilizer for the many kinds of vegetables that eventually found their way back to the city markets. This form of disposing of human waste made it impossible to eat any raw vegetables; everything had to be boiled. Leafy vegetables like lettuce were totally avoided. The water supply, too, was highly contaminated and had to be boiled before consumption. As there was only a single cold-water tap in our house, daily bathing meant washing from a basin filled with hot water boiled in a kettle heated on a small primitive charcoal-burning clay stove. Mama made sure that there was enough hot water for us everyday. I was kept extremely clean. It was an obsession for Mama to make sure I was scrupulously washed and my thick curly hair thoroughly combed every night and inspected for head lice.

As if the ambient noise of the ghetto was not enough, our family was caught between two warring couples who shared the house with us. A young woman and her abusive husband, who had a fondness for drink, rented the other ground floor room. Mr. and Mrs. Prokosch, Polish Jews, who got along as well as the proverbial cat and dog, occupied the two rooms upstairs. The Prokosch's favourite pastime was to fight at all hours of the day. I found this all very disturbing because I had never known anything but harmony between Mama and Papa. I had never heard them raise their voices, even during some kind of disagreement. The very idea of a man and a woman constantly fighting and bickering came as a shock to me.

In keeping with the tense atmosphere in the house, there was constant warfare between Mama and Mrs. Prokosch over the use of the kitchen. I did not like Mrs. Prokosch at all. I do not think she was very fond of me, either. The ongoing feud between Mama and Mrs. Prokosch was actually as ridiculous as could be; Mama spoke no Polish, and Mrs. Prokosch spoke no German or English. They yelled and screamed at each other in their respective languages, which no doubt added to their frustration because they never resolved anything. Eventually, they picked up on each other's key words and phrases of insults and hurled them back and forth. At least they did not get physical, for which we were all thankful. At night, when Papa and Opa were home, there seemed to be a truce. But when she was not arguing with Mama, Mrs. Prokosch got into it with Mr. Prokosch regardless of the time of day. The feuding was never-ending.

I did like the young lady on the ground floor, however. Her name was Yetty Gross. She spent a lot of time with us, probably to get away from her mean husband. Yetty was very nice to me, and I felt sad when he yelled at her. She was Mama's age and they became very best friends. It would be a lifelong friendship that was brought to an end by Mama's death decades later. With the encouragement of Mama and Papa, Yetty eventually extricated herself from the miserable relationship she was in and later remarried, much more happily. She and her new husband would eventually settle in San Francisco.

Yetty Gross

The number of schools available in the Hongkew ghetto was quite limited. Despite what appeared to be a hopeless future for children, the adult world still put value on their education. One such institution of learning was the four-room Freysinger's Jewish Elementary and Middle School, in which I was enrolled. The school was located a few blocks from where we lived, which in my mind was about the only thing good about it. I made my daily, reluctant journey to this unhappy place, sustained only by the knowledge that after school I was free again. My classmates and I were taught in crowded and ill-equipped classrooms. It was far from an ideal knowledge-absorbing environment. Recess was spent in a narrow laneway that led to the school. It could hardly be called a playground, but that was its purpose. I spent a lot of time daydreaming about being outside-about having adventures. To me, it seemed that I was not getting much of an education in this school at all. Learning how to read was one of the main focuses of the curriculum, but I already knew how to do that.

The other learning institution in Hongkew was the one built by the wealthy Kadoorie family. It was established especially for the schooling of refugee children. The school was palatial in comparison to the Freysinger School and the envy of all who were unable to go there. Education for older European children, at high school level or beyond, could be obtained only by privately hiring experienced tutors or academicians. Schools for the foreign community were not supported by public funds; therefore, the quality of education depended wholly upon what a family could afford. Many parents tutored their children at home. I, too, learned a lot at home from Mama and Opa.

Freysinger's Jewish Elementary- and Middle School

Report for the term ending July 7th 1944

Name Heinemann, Hannelore. Actual attendance Regular

Form I Number of times late

Age at end of term 8 · yrs. 5 Order Good

SUBJECTS	REMARKS	TEACHERS
Hebrew		
Scripture	Most satisfactory.	Miss Cohn
Jewish History		
Grammar	Satisfactory	Mr. Wolff
Composition	Good	Mr. Wolff
Reading	Very Good	Mr. Wolff
Dictation	Good	Mr. Wolff
Recitation	very good	Miss Cohn
Geometry		
~~French~~ Writing	Satisfactory	Miss Cohn
Arithmetic	Most satisfactory	Mr. Freysinger
Geography		
History / Biology } General Knowledge	Satisfactory	Miss Cohn
Drawing	Not satisfactory	Miss Cohn
Needlework		
Physical Exercises	Satisfactory	Miss Cohn
Singing	Fairly Good	Miss Cohn

Conduct good

General Remarks

Freysinger
FORM MASTER

Ismar Freysinger
HEAD MASTER

School will reassemble on August 1st at [illegible]

Freysinger's Jewish Elementary and Middle School report card, July 7, 1944

It seemed to me that they knew more than Mr. Freysinger, but that was probably because they taught me stuff I was interested in. And, there was the ultimate open-air school, which was my favourite: the streets of the city, the school of life!

The extreme climate that was endemic to Shanghai made the daily trip to school particularly difficult in the summer and in the winter. No matter how warm my hand-knitted socks or gloves were, frostbite was my constant companion in the cold-weather months. My hands and feet were red and inflamed with open sores. Perhaps the lack of proper nourishment, or my thin little body, made this discomfort inevitable. Nothing Mama did alleviated this condition. In the asphalt-melting summers, which were humid beyond belief, the agony of severe cases of athlete's foot plagued both Papa and me. Shanghailanders aptly named this malady "Hong Kong Foot," while residents of Hong Kong referred to it as "Shanghai Foot." In my case, it required daily attention by lancing each and every water-filled pustule, followed by the stinging application of some purple ointment. It was a painful ordeal, and every night poor Mama performed this routine to the accompaniment of my howls of pain. She tried to distract me by singing my favourite songs or telling me stories. When Mama was not up to entertaining me, Opa pitched in by relating some of his great stories or singing old army songs. Sometimes I was kept in bed during the more severe bouts of this ailment. When I was able to go to school, I had to wear bandages and socks to keep my feet free from the dust and dirt of the streets.

Shortly after our return to Hongkew, Opa became involved with the already established Chevra Kadisha, the burial society of the Jewish Community. He now felt an even greater need to be more actively involved in religious matters and to express his faith by being of service to others. The Chevra Kadisha was an important group as it made sure all burials were conducted in strict keeping with Jewish precepts. As the years slipped by, the society was kept busy.

Meanwhile, Papa worked hard to maintain his beloved book business in the French Concession. Now that we were back in Hongkew, he spent three to four hours each day cycling to and from the Western Arts Gallery. He never complained and would have travelled twice as far to keep his store open if necessary. "We are fortunate to have this business, and I must do everything to ensure it remains open; and that means putting up with the inconvenience of getting there and back," he would tell Mama whenever she asked him to try and spend some more time at home. He earned enough money to feed and house his own family, as well as help support a few others who were not as fortunate.

Papa, who had never been a church-going man until now, was instrumental in founding a Protestant Association devoted to and working for the few German Protestant families who also found themselves living in Hongkew. Perhaps it was Opa's devotion to his faith and service to others that inspired Papa. Maybe he had been galvanized into action because he felt he had been blessed with the safety of his family. His adherence to the Lutheran religion was further testimony to the influence that his stepmother Feodora had on him years ago. I, meanwhile, was raised in two faiths. On Sundays, Papa would take me to the Lutheran services conducted by the Reverend Pastor Wedel. Opa took it upon himself to keep me versed in Judaism.

Opa and Mama, as well as Papa, observed all Jewish customs without fail. For me, the most distinctive was the Friday night Sabbath ceremony. With its festive flickering candles, home-baked bread, and the joyous Kiddish, all presided over by Opa, our room became a warm protective cocoon harbouring us in a time of trouble. For most refugees, their faith and religion were the only things they had left. It was something to which they could cling, something with which they could face life and death.

Even as a seven-year-old child, I was aware of the existence of such miserable conditions as those in Hongkew. The very closeness and lack of privacy of our quarters made it impossible for me not to overhear the conversations of my parents and their friends. The small community of Hongkew was rife with rumour and gossip. The circulation of such stories and minutiae of daily life were thrived upon, the more horrendous the better. I, as well as many others, young though we were, could not be protected or kept from knowing about these miseries that were everywhere. A simple outing on the streets exposed one to beggars of all ages. They were dressed in filthy rags and were barefoot or else were wearing flimsy sandals tied to the feet with twine. Insistently, the beggars stopped anyone who passed, thin bony hands stretched out hoping to receive a few pennies. If they were ignored, they picked some of the multitudes of lice off their bodies and threw them at those who held back. It was not unusual to see the lifeless body of some poor soul lying on a cracked sidewalk, later to be collected and disposed of who knows where.

The atmosphere of the street was charged. The air was pungent with an amalgam of food being cooked, unwashed bodies in unwashed clothes, the exhaust of motorized vehicles, and the smell of the river: these were the distinct smells of life and death. People rushed around everywhere or hovered in the shadows like condemned prisoners hoping for a reprieve. Rickshaw and pedicab operators darted in and out of traffic. Vendors of all kinds plotted out space on the crowded sidewalks. In time, the more needy Jews would be seen competing with Chinese vendors for customers on some of the busier streets.

The sidewalks of Kungping Road were where most of the refugees congregated to sell their belongings. It was a favourite destination for the more affluent Chinese citizens seeking highly valued European treasures. Displayed on blankets spread out on the sidewalk were items ranging from the miniscule, including rings and fountain pens, to larger pieces, such as furniture. Even lingerie, as well as leather and fur coats were for sale. Then, when everything was gone, the blanket would be sold, too. Without the prospect of gainful employment, these refugee vendors were fortunate in a way: they were able to sell or barter the possessions they had been able to get out of Europe in order to help insure their survival in Shanghai, at least for the short term. Eventually, most of them would join the thousands who relied on soup kitchens for a daily meal.

Living conditions in Hongkew exacerbated every

health problem so that even minor ailments became serious medical situations. The most threatening were the epidemic diseases like cholera and typhus. Though outbursts did occur, particularly in the overcrowded Heime, the Japanese authorities countered this by ordering frequent inoculations in which all citizens had to participate on a regular basis. Although the fear of an epidemic was always present, the authorities were successful in their strict application of the rules. Everyone was issued a small card that indicated they were vaccinated. Failure to produce this card on demand immediately resulted in another injection, no matter what the excuse.

Staffed by refugee doctors and nurses, there were three hospitals in operation in Hongkew. The skills and expertise of these medical personnel, formerly some of the best in Europe, were daily put to the test by performing miracles without proper surgical instruments or adequate medical supplies. Operating under very primitive conditions, doctors had to be innovative and practise the sort of medicine they would not have dared dream about back in Europe. Still, they managed to save quite a few lives.

Despite the daily rigours of survival, life in the Hongkew ghetto took on some of the aspects of European culture thought to have been left behind. Even though conditions were harsh, Jewish life flourished. Refugees opened bakeries, cafés, nightclubs, newspapers, and journals. Birthdays and holidays were celebrated, anniversaries remembered, and there were weddings and Bar Mitzvot by the score. Well-known musicians and other performers found that they could put their artistic training to good use in a variety of ways and were able to earn enough to at least stay alive. Nearly all of the places offering entertainment were able to provide live bands, the latest music, and cabaret acts with talent that would have been the envy of any large European city. The restaurants, coffeehouses, and nightclubs were frequented not only by fun-loving refugees but also Japanese officers and other nationals. Somehow the owners of these establishments were able to offer fine food, even though rationing was in effect. There was colourful and engaging all-night entertainment, curfews notwithstanding. Wherever there were resourceful people, wheeling and dealing knew no boundaries. Stories of intrigue and high-powered doings abounded. Crime and corruption were everywhere, but the citizens of the city did not think in those terms, they considered it a way of life and moved along with the current.

The Japanese, using refugee work-gangs, had rebuilt and repaired some of the damage they had inflicted upon Hongkew in 1937. Some of the repaired streets, like busy Chusan Road, accommodated small stores that offered a variety of goods and services. On Muirhead Road, there stood a large two-storey building that housed the central market for the ghetto. This building was covered by a roof, open on all sides and supported by pillars. On the ground floor were Chinese vendors selling vegetables from outlying farms; questionable meat from slaughtered cows, pigs and chickens; clothing; sundries; and other items. On the second floor, Europeans able to manufacture edible delicacies and other assorted items sold their goods.

In all kinds of weather, Mama patiently lined up at a distribution centre for food, which was scarce and rationed. A very poor quality of margarine was doled out in small quantities. A few handfuls of hardened brown lumps passed for sugar. Yellowed flour, riddled with insects, had to be sieved in order to avoid the extra protein.

Sometimes, I accompanied Mama on her daily trip to the market, where quite often she bought a small amount of homemade sauerkraut from a Polish lady. It was the best sauerkraut I had ever eaten. The thought of which still produces puddles on my tongue. Our walk home was made more enjoyable by the contented crunchy munching of this delicious purchase.

Mama did all of her cooking on the little clay stove in the kitchen which she shared with Mrs. Prokosch and Yetty. She considered herself fortunate to have a place to cook. Many of the residents of Hongkew had no such luxury and did their cooking in the congested laneways, no matter what the weather. Although meal preparation without proper cooking facilities was a real challenge, Mama still managed to bring hearty and delicious European dishes to the table with the few wartime ingredients available. Her ingenuity as a cook ensured that Papa, who in former days loved his marzipan, still got a bit of this tasty sweet on his birthday by using sweet yams and a few precious drops of almond extract to the base mixture. Even though the end product was a bright yellow, Papa was in seventh heaven. It was the little things that seemed to please him the most.

Whenever Mama and I went on errands, we passed one of the larger Heime. She never failed to remind me that I was forbidden to set foot in the place. She warned me of the dangers of catching some horrible disease and other dire possibilities. I, of course, chose to ignore her well-meaning warnings, as I was always curious about these forbidden places. Through my daily adventures, I made friends with children who lived under truly miserable conditions in the Heime. When they invited me inside, I never hesitated. Together we wandered through the large rooms, crowded with row upon row of two- and three-decker bunk beds. Steamer trunks served as tables and as storage for belongings. Everything was in the open; no nooks, crannies, or little hiding places existed in these windowless rooms. At all times of the day, people languished on their beds. Many were weakened by hunger and victimized by inescapable melancholia. There simply was no reason to get up. The reek of stale food, unwashed bodies, and mouldy clothing was pervasive. The sounds of muffled groans and the clearing of throat, nasal, and other bodily passages dominated. The residents, as well as the visitors, had learned to ignore all this and go about their business. In most cases, their business was simply to stay alive.

Soup kitchens run by women and outside volunteers provided skimpy, basic meals, which were just enough to keep one from starvation. The Jewish Community raised the money required for this mealtime operation. As the war progressed, it became harder and harder to keep up with the demand for food, and so a number of people already weakened by hunger and disease did not survive. Even as young as I was, the difference of my lifestyle compared to that of my friends confined in such a place was obvious. In the midst of all this hardship, enterprising people made their lives not only bearable but also comfortable. By sheer bravado and imagination, or possibly good fortune, some lived out the war and managed to enrich themselves. Others were not as fortunate, and for them the daily litany of misery became more strident. A significant number of people faced starvation and illness, caused by the unsanitary living conditions in Hongkew. Some succumbed to the emotional effect of hopelessness that pervaded the ghetto. Everything took its toll on the population of Hongkew.

Towards the end of 1943, a letter from Opa's brother, Berthold, who had remained behind in Berlin, somehow reached us. It contained the ominous news that he was among the Jews being rounded up by the Nazis under the order of "resettlement." Opa was very disturbed by this. He assumed that since writing the letter, the date of which was unclear, Berthold and his family had already been transported to a place they would never be heard from again. Berthold's parting words in the letter were: "Do not expect to see us again." They knew what awaited them. "Resettlement" was the kiss of death. Shortly after the war we would be overjoyed to receive news from Berthold's children, Alfred and Hansi. They had survived the camps as slave labourers and had been able to make their way to a new life in New Zealand.

Meanwhile, the dark days and nights of war continued. After having won a decisive naval battle at Midway Island in June 1942, the Americans had kept pushing east towards Japan. They gradually liberated island after island in the Pacific Ocean, reaching Okinawa in April 1945. Everyone expected hostilities to make their way to Shanghai and, in preparation for the inevitable air raids, curfews and blackouts were ordered in Hongkew. Patrolling Japanese soldiers, sometimes accompanied by chosen members of the Jewish Committee, walked the lanes and streets of the ghetto. They were especially vigilant for any light that might escape through curtains from the not completely darkened rooms. The discovery of such unavoidable mishaps resulted in loud poundings on the doors and threats of punishment. In order to comply, Mama had sewn thick black curtains to cover the window facing the tiny courtyard. Many long evenings were spent playing cards with friends by the dim light of the radio dial or a kerosene lamp burning low. One such visitor was Horst Levine. Like many of Papa's friends, Horst had come into our lives via the Western Arts Gallery. Mr. Levine was a bit of a local celebrity who worked as a columnist for one of the many Shanghai newspapers and as a radio announcer.

On stifling hot summer nights, it became necessary for my family to leave our uncomfortable room. We would sit on the sidewalks just to get the slightest breath of cool air. Opa and I often sat in the dark together as he told me Germanic hero tales. Sometimes he spoke of his wartime experiences. Many of the stories I had heard before, and some were new; but Opa had a never-ending reservoir of material to keep me fascinated. With all lights extinguished, the stars presented a dazzling canopy that even the war and the authorities could not dim.

On other nights the stars were eclipsed by the nightly aerial displays of powerful searchlights that constantly revolved around the sky looking for their elusive prey. The beautiful strobe light displays spun their deadly webs until they transfixed the object of their search. Then, sounding like many sharp barks, the volleys of anti-aircraft fire lit up the sky on their way to bringing down the enemy.

Daylight air raids were becoming more of a reality. During these air raids, we huddled in the concrete-walled kitchen with the other occupants of the house, believing this to be a safe haven from the bombs. Although Hongkew would not escape American bombardment, I am happy to say that our naive belief system regarding the safety of our quasi-shelter was never put to the test.

One Saturday, in the summer of 1944, Opa rose early to prepare for his weekly walk to the synagogue for Sabbath services. He was a faithful attendant at one of the three synagogues in Hongkew. Being a devout Jew he carefully observed all the Sabbath rules, to which I was not expected to adhere. Even though Opa prized his religion, he respected the fact that it would be up to me to make an eventual choice between Judaism and Christianity. I heard him get up and shuffle around. Because this particular day was a special day, I was too excited to stay in bed. Peter Flusser, the older brother of my best friend, Erika, was celebrating his seventeenth birthday. I was invited to be her guest at the party. "My goodness you are up early today, Hannelore. Are you going to accompany me to the synagogue?" he jokingly asked. I told him about the birthday party and he gave me an understanding smile. "Well you make sure you have a good time," he said and departed. I impatiently waited for the morning, which was giving way to a hot humid day, to go by.

The Flussers were well-to-do Hongkew residents who had an entire three-storey house for their home. They lived just a few blocks away from us, and I spent many happy hours playing with Erika and her large collection of toys.

On this special day there would be extra cookies, candies, and cake. In the afternoon, all decked out in party finery, I was finally allowed to depart. As always when I'm having a lot of fun, the time flew by. Some hours later, Erika's mother told me it was time to go. "Don't linger on the streets and go straight home because it will be curfew soon," she reminded me. I thanked her and Erika for having me over and set out for Alcock Road. As daylight turned into dusk, I hurried home along the deserted streets in order to beat the curfew. Across the street, a little ahead of me, a stooped figure of a man with long sideburns, clearly a devout Jew, also hurried to meet the curfew deadline. He shuffled along, totally absorbed in his own space with his eyes riveted on the ground ahead of him. The old timer failed to notice a Japanese officer, regally dressed in full uniform and sword, passing by him. He did not respectfully bow to the officer as per required etiquette. I heard a shout from the officer and, before the hapless object of his anger could react, the shiny sword was removed from its scabbard. It flashed through the air and effectively decapitated the man. For a brief moment the scene appeared surreal to me; it happened so quickly. The blood emanating from the man's severed jugular, and his liberated head rolling on the sidewalk were too graphic to be dismissed as a figment of my imagination. A stunned moment later I turned tail and scurried out of sight not wishing to be recognized as a witness to this brutally shocking event. Not only did the family of this helpless victim suffer a great loss, but I, at that moment, suffered a loss of some of my childhood innocence. I had seen dead bodies before, but this was the first time I was exposed to such a callous life-ending act.

My membership in the Protestant community in Hongkew was formalized when Mama and Papa had me baptized. This was done, presumably, in the naive belief that somehow a person who was baptized might be exempt from future harassment or extermination. Years later, I questioned this wisdom as baptism had not kept Papa off any Nazi lists targeting Jews in Germany. But there were other benefits for me as a member of the Protestant Church. I was invited to join the children's choir. Because I liked singing and entertaining people, being in the choir suited me just fine. The little choir was actually quite good, and we were called upon to perform on various holidays and other church functions. I particularly enjoyed the Christmas parties, complete with Santa and presents. At one such grand Christmas occasion, the choir sang its well-rehearsed carols with particular aplomb. We were rewarded with candies, home-baked Christmas cookies, and sweets. These were a real luxury and something I could never get my fill of. I was also thrilled to receive on that occasion, along with the edible goodies, a doll almost as big as myself. Toys were a scarce commodity in Hongkew and not something money was spent on by the impoverished refugee community. Most children had no toys and were resigned to play with whatever they could. In addition to my small dolly, Lisa, and stuffed lion, Zoltar, which had come with me from Berlin and were still among my prized possessions, I had only a ball and a few homemade toys. One of these was a cardboard box Opa had converted into a dollhouse, which was furnished with crude little furniture he had made of tiny scraps of wood.

The doll I had received at the church party was heaven-sent, and I hung on to her the rest of the night thinking I would never let her go.

Protestant Church play, 1942/1943
Hannelore: first row, second from right

On that wonderful Christmas it had snowed the entire day. As Papa and I quietly made our way home from the celebrations on the crisp, cold, clear night that followed, the snow lay untrodden on the silent, darkened streets. My doll was securely clutched in one hand, while Papa firmly clutched the other. The stars hung in the heavens above with a myriad jewelled brightness. Total blackout was already in effect and the awe-inspiring display above us was the only source of light. Those truly magical moments became etched in my memory. I especially treasured such occasions with Papa because I saw so little of him during those trying times.

One of Papa's immediate family members who had made her way to Shanghai to seek refuge was his biological mother, Lotte. Papa and his mother had become estranged after my paternal grandfather, Richard Heinemann, remarried the sympathetic and noble Feodora von Buggenhagen. Papa's already acrimonious relationship with his mother deteriorated even further in Shanghai when he learned that she had hatched a plan to kidnap me for a ransom. Papa confronted her as soon as he heard about this and, consequently, her ill-conceived scheme never took root. Despite her wicked intentions to extort money from Papa, he felt a moral obligation towards her and made sure she had enough money to survive on while in Shanghai. There certainly was no love lost between them. When she told him she wanted to get to know her granddaughter, Papa drew the line. He warned her to stay away from not just me but the entire family, and I was under strict orders to avoid her at all costs.

Lotte was a small, purposeful woman with bright blond hair, whom I occasionally encountered on my travels. Whenever I did, I hurried across the street to avoid her. In a way this avoidance was troublesome for me, as I did not fully grasp the estrangement between her and Papa. I knew she was my grandmother who, other than my beloved Opa Silberstein, was the only living grandparent I had. I would have liked to have had an Oma, and it seemed like the hand of fate brought us all together in Hongkew. Still, I understood that there was such a thing as family politics and I accepted the situation. Eventually I forgot about her, and her name was no longer brought up in our household. She would leave Shanghai after the war, and I would never see her again.

LIFE UNDER MR. GHOYA

The diminutive form of Kano Ghoya, simply known to his Jewish charges as "Mr. Ghoya," personified the influence of the ever-present Japanese authorities on our daily lives. This military police sergeant had been given control over the Jewish community and its affairs, and he reported only to the Director General at the Office of Stateless Refugees Affairs, Mr. Kubota Tsutomu. Mr. Ghoya, who was no more than five-foot-five in height, sported a Hitleresque moustache and strutted around the streets of his little fiefdom like a peacock on parade. Anyone wishing to leave the confines of the ghetto needed to apply for a permit which had to be shown to the border sentries upon departure and return to the district. On any given day, from eight o'clock in the morning until noon, one could find long lines of nervous applicants stretched around the block leading to Mr. Ghoya's office. There were two types of permits for which one could apply: the easily obtained day pass, and the more difficult long-term pass for those who worked or conducted business outside of Hongkew. Despite their name, the long-term passes had a narrow time limit and needed to be renewed every two weeks. This expiration required the applicants to appear in person before Mr. Ghoya for his approval.

Ghoya, however, was prone to a particular nervousness in front of tall people, which often proved to be a liability for those who were not vertically challenged. He was subject to varying moods, sometimes so foul that shouting and face-slapping were in store for anyone appearing before him. He occasionally jumped on his desk, waved a ruler, and announced he was "King of the Jews." Anyone unfortunate enough to be standing in line on such days was very quickly informed by the departing victims of what was in store for them. As nearly all applicants depended on these permits to conduct business outside the ghetto in order to support themselves and their families, this uncertainty every two weeks was difficult to live with. Papa, however, was not a tall man and did not have to worry about Ghoya's penchant for humiliating or discriminating against those who were. Papa had one other thing going for him that greatly facilitated the acquisition of the biweekly passes: he had been able to acquire from the French Consulate General in Shanghai a letter asking the Japanese authorities to allow him to travel freely between Hongkew and his store in the Concession because his expertise in bibliographical research was of value to members of the French community.

Like so many people of the Far East who loved and indulged young children, Ghoya, too, had a friendly tolerance toward the very young. It was therefore not uncommon for men who felt vulnerable to take their own or other people's children on their appointments for the pass renewals. Thanks to his idiosyncrasies and histrionics, Ghoya was destined to become one of the most infamous personalities of the Japanese occupying forces in Shanghai.

CONSULAT GÉNÉRAL DE FRANCE
A
CHANG-HAI

Mr. Heinz-Egon HEINEMANN, manager of the "Western Arts Gallery", 1166 Avenue Joffre, is going to live in Hongkew following the prescriptions decreed by the Japanese Authorities.

Mr. Heinz-Egon HEINEMANN bringing, because of his special professional training received in the cultural centers of Germany, a very valuable and irreplaceable collaboration in bibliographical research work to many members of the French Colony, the French Consulate General would be grateful to the Japanese Authorities if they would permit him to come freely to Shanghai every day.

Mr. HEINEMANN had addressed a petition to that effect on the 3rd April 1943 which was registered under the number 207./.

Shanghai, 4th May 1943.

Consulat Général de France a Chang-hai letter, May 4, 1943

During his tenure in Shanghai Mr. Ghoya was one of the most talked about figures. Many stories circulated, but one of the most memorable concerned a devout Jew, complete with sidelocks and yarmulke, who pleaded for a pass. Ghoya looked at him for a long moment, then beckoned him to approach and whispered into his ear. "How much is the gold dollar today?" he queried the man. Dealing in American currency was punishable by instant execution so this was a loaded question to be asked. The applicant hesitated for only a moment, then beckoned Ghoya to approach and whispered back into his ear, "Do you wish to buy, or do you wish to sell, Mr. Ghoya?" Ghoya laughed loudly, being in a good mood that day, and handed the man a pass.

Another popular story that circulated in the ghetto was about the misadventure of a young refugee who befriended a group of Japanese officers at a nightclub. As the evening progressed he and the officers got quite inebriated and it was decided that the young man should accompany the officers after the club closed for more drinking at their quarters. However, the officers were quartered outside the ghetto borders and the young man had no pass. Insisting that he accompany them anyway, they approached a border checkpoint and ordered the sentries to let him through. Not only did the sentries obey the orders of the officers, they were made to bow to the white refugee in order to show their respect. In the early morning hours he was driven home; but in the more sobering days that followed, the young man realized the events of that night had made it impossible for him ever to go near the ghetto borders again. He feared encountering the same guards and at the very least be subjected to a severe beating by them to compensate for their earlier humiliation.

Most of these stories, rumours, gossip, and the latest war news were passed around through the many newspapers that were published in Shanghai. An active radio station kept inhabitants informed, misinformed, amused, agitated, or depressed. All these methods of communication and spreading of information were vital to the survival of the Jewish community. Listening to short-wave radio, however, was the only means of getting non-biased news, and this activity was strictly forbidden for all residents of Shanghai. In various nightclubs and cabarets, clever skits often amused patrons. The authorities and Hongkew celebrities were often the butt of these skits. These were thinly disguised so not to offend and thereby land the perpetrators in the infamous Ward Road Jail. Some of the less risqué skits were based on nostalgic memories of former good times in Europe.

Confrontation with the occupying forces was in the cards for just about everyone at one time or another. Occasionally, to assert their authority and power, the Japanese issued an order for a surprise street round up, which the ghetto community could not avoid. Groups of soldiers would cordon off a busy street and everyone found there was stopped, questioned, and searched. Sometimes someone was marched off, presumably for further questioning or because he or she was suspected of having committed an offence, real or imagined. These raids were called "Razias" and occurred without warning; anyone attempting to escape was beaten, if they were lucky. Although the Razias were mostly met with humour and acceptance, they contributed to a life that was already stressful and always on the verge of danger.

Throughout 1943 and 1944, there were renewed diplomatic efforts by the Hitler regime to persuade the Japanese government to bring the "Final Solution" into effect. Still, despite the diplomatic pressure put upon them by the Nazis, and the Nazis' promise to help build the necessary death camps, the Japanese continued to reject the repeated requests of their Axis partners. To the Japanese, the Jews remained stateless middle-European refugees, racially no different from their German allies. Furthermore, the Jews were not at war with the Japanese. To the Japanese sensibilities, the extermination of old men, women, and children was beyond reasoning. In fact, the Japanese saw themselves as the protectors of the Jewish population in Hongkew and wanted no part of the Nazis' murderous plan.

This precarious wartime climate and constant worry about my safety had especially taken its toll on Mama's health. Opa's preoccupation with his duties to the Jewish Community, in addition to Papa's long hours away from home, had left her with the responsibility of looking after an adventurous eight-year-old who was always wandering off and was mostly up to no good. Accordingly, Mama and Papa arranged to place me in the care of Frau Misch, a cantankerous elderly woman who freelanced as a nanny/tutor of sorts. Frau Misch was a fierce despot and was very fast with a ruler across the knuckles; in the eyes of Mama and Papa, she was the perfect candidate to curtail my activities.

My frequent complaints and tears had little effect, either on the perpetrator or Mama.

The issue of my discipline was a conflicting concern in our household. When caught during some childish misdeed, which happened often enough, the threats of receiving a spanking from Papa when he came home at night resulted in my earnest apologies and promises of improved behaviour. The threats were then withdrawn. From time to time Papa, however, felt obliged to take me into the kitchen to dole out some kind of punishment. He was a gentle person and abhorred violence; by mutual agreement he produced a loud slapping noise, which was accompanied by the appropriate howls of pain from me! Although Mama would sometimes spank me, depending on my transgression, the more usual punishment was my being made to stand in the corner with my back to the room.

Frau Misch had good moments, however. In order to give Mama her much needed rest, the elderly lady took me on long walks when the weather was fine. Although I preferred the company of Opa, who now was too busy with his own life, the outings with Frau Misch were fun enough. We often went to one of the prettier gardens attached to the largest medical facility, the Ward Road Hospital, where I enjoyed playing among the well-tended flowerbeds. It reminded me a little of the garden paradises of the French Concession. Hongkew, unfortunately, did not have many such oases but there was a small park with swings, a slide, and a sandbox. It was usually quite busy, filled by people wishing to escape the dirty, narrow, and crowded streets.

Illo Koratkowski and Ernest Heppner's wedding in April 1945 was, like all weddings in the ghetto, an extra reason to remain hopeful that there was a future to live for and a reason for celebration. I was looking forward to their big day not only because weddings always meant a little extra food had been scrounged up for the occasion but because I had been asked to be a flower girl. Unfortunately, as fate would have it, I came down with the measles and Mama and Papa attended the service and celebration without me. But their wedding and my illness were quickly forgotten when American bombers began to attack Japanese targets around Shanghai a short while later.

The fear that the ghetto might not escape the destructive raids became ever more a reality. The Japanese had strategically placed some of their wartime industrial plants and other important military installations around and near Hongkew. Also nearby were the prisoner of war camps that housed enemy aliens including American and British citizens. This planning was done with the belief that allied bombers would be reluctant to target any area that would endanger the lives of either the refugees or their own people. As the war progressed and the pressure on the allies mounted to bring hostilities with Japan to a speedy end, the intensity and increased frequency of these destructive raids occurred with the resultant loss of lives.

The residents of Hongkew had become used to the daily whine of air-raid sirens although some public shelters existed, our family never made use of them. Instead we chose to huddle in our little concrete-walled kitchen which would not have saved us even from near-misses, never mind if a bomb had found its way through our roof.

June and July of 1945 were exceptionally inclement, keeping the bombers at bay. But on July 17th, the day was sunny and clear. Just before noon on that morning, Opa was on the balcony of our Alcock Road home when his attention was drawn to a droning in the far off distance. He feared the worst and was on his way downstairs when the air raid sirens sent their strident warnings of approaching aircraft. Minutes later the first frightening sounds of the booming impact of bombs shook the Hongkew area. The house we occupied swayed, and a gentle rain of plaster descended from the ceiling. As the drone of low-flying planes drew closer so did the anxiety-inducing thudding sound of exploding bombs. It did not take long for the planes to head off again, the horror of the raid seemed to last an eternity. Their departure happened as quickly as their arrival. The all-clear sirens eventually followed the silence. As people emerged from their homes into the sunlit streets to see what was left of their neighbourhood, the extent of the damage quickly became clear.

As we ventured outside to inspect the destruction, we noticed that several blocks nearby had been hit. Fortunately, we were spared. Many of the hastily repaired residential buildings, which were damaged during the Japanese invasion of 1937, had collapsed like houses of cards. The Tongshan Road communal kitchen was also damaged. Throughout Hongkew, dozens of refugees had been killed and hundreds had sustained injuries of various magnitudes. Thousands were homeless.

The casualties were placed in or on any available vehicle and transported to the nearest hospital. People rushed to the damaged areas to rescue shrapnel-wounded victims and those buried in the rubble. The dead were laid out in rows, covered over, and later removed for burial. Frantic people searched for loved ones, whereas others mourned over friends and family. I was appalled by what I saw and had a hard time reconciling myself with the harsh reality of the senseless destruction and the snuffing out of innocent life.

As I wandered around the neighbourhood in a semi-trance, I suddenly found myself at a nearby bombed-out house. The sound of moaning drew me to a pile of rubble. Upon closer investigation, I saw an arm protruding. I wanted to help this buried person and grabbed the hand to tug on it. To my horror I found that I was holding a detached limb. I could not imagine what I had done and, as my loud calls for help brought people running, I handed the arm to the first person to reach me and I ran off. This incident, like the beheading of the old Jew, was among the most traumatic events I endured in Shanghai. The images of that day would resurface as nightmares for years to come.

In the weeks that followed the bombing, refugee work gangs, pressed into service by the Japanese, undertook a massive cleanup operation. While this was an unpleasant task, it did create an area of focus and took the minds of those at work off their own misery. No doubt that some considered themselves lucky to be among the living, while others looked at the dead as the lucky ones who had been delivered from this living hell. Bodies were extracted from the ruins, and bombed-out sites were cleared. Rebuilding efforts, however, were hampered by continued bad weather. We discovered later it was exactly this inclement weather that spared us from being visited again by the feared bombers.

In order to help house those left homeless by the raid, Jewish communal organisations petitioned Director General of Stateless Refugees Affairs, Kubota Tsutomu, to lift the containment of refugees from Hongkew so they could resettle in other parts of the city. Their appeal fell on deaf ears. Although my family was spared from the destruction, the bombing did affect me in a very personal way. One of the families whose home was destroyed in the raid was that of my friend Erika Flusser. She and her family escaped the carnage, but her brother Peter was not spared injury. He had been caught sleeping in his second-floor bedroom when the raid began. The concussive impact of a bomb that dropped nearby caused the entire floor of the house to collapse to ground level. He miraculously survived with his life intact, but a piece of shrapnel entered his knee. This wound resulted in the eventual amputation of the leg. As with many tragedies, some good fortune would come out of this. After the war Peter and his family were among the first to be able to emigrate to the United States so that he would be able to receive further treatments for his wounds. It was a heavy price to pay for a ticket to America.

Shortly after dawn in early September 1945, yelling and noise from outside woke me from my sleep. I launched myself out of bed, thinking another air raid was in progress. Opa ran to me, picked me up, and loudly announced that the war had ended. I did not immediately understand the momentous impact of this news, but that night the streets were filled with celebrants. No Japanese soldiers or police officers were in sight. It was if they had evaporated into thin air. No doubt, if they were out and about they would have been lynched by the mob that took over the ghetto.

Prisoners in the internment camps woke up to find the places deserted. The Japanese guards had left. In the ghetto, Japanese store owners had abandoned their shops. In the days that followed, the Japanese, who were technically still in power and in charge, kept a very circumspect profile. In those times of uncertainty, while waiting for the Chinese authorities to return to power and for the arrival of the American armed forces, instances of looting and general lawlessness occurred. Even though people were aware of the horrific details of the atomic bombings of Hiroshima and Nagasaki, which had brought the war in the Pacific to an end, the immediate reaction was one of relief.

The next few weeks saw the arrival of the triumphant Americans, the release of Japanese-held prisoners, the improvement of living conditions, and the influx of relief groups, including the Red Cross and some Jewish organizations. With their arrival came much needed food and clothing. The heartbreaking task of tracing lost relatives in Europe also began in earnest. The survival of those who had not escaped the Nazis became more and more doubtful as people began to hear of the horrific details regarding the death camps of Europe. In the cinemas, stunning newsreels preceded American movies, such as *Fantasia* and *Gone With The Wind*, showing the concentration camps being liberated by the Allies and the gruesome scenes that met the soldiers' eyes. The walls of Hongkew became papered with long lists of Holocaust names, placed there by the Red Cross and Jewish agencies.

Heart-wrenching stories emerged from the reports of the Red Cross, whose efforts to reunite families often ended in failure and tragedy. One of these stories concerned a couple with whom my family was acquainted. They had set the wheels in motion to find a son left behind in Holland, where they had taken the child from Germany after the events of Kristallnacht. They had done so in the belief that it was safe to leave him in the temporary care of a family they knew. This family had already taken a few other children under their wing with the promise they would be well looked after. The plan was to retrieve their son upon leaving Europe; but they had been unable to do this, and they spent the war years surviving in Shanghai with the hope of being reunited with their boy. The Red Cross eventually uncovered the tragic story that the boy's caregivers, thinking they could save their own family, had given up the children to the Gestapo. The betrayal of the children had not saved the family, however, and they were also sent to their deaths. The mother of the boy, upon receiving this news, lost her sanity and died from grief. The aftermath of World War II was fraught with many such devastating accounts.

Those who received no news about loved ones left behind kept hoping against hope that their own story would have a happy ending. We were one of those families who lived in uncertainty regarding our extended family members. It took some time before we were informed that the children of Opa's brother, Berthold, had survived the camps. While the real numbers of casualties from the Holocaust were not known right away, it became quickly apparent to the Shanghai refugees that hundreds of thousands and possibly even millions of their fellow Jews had perished in a nightmare they had been fortunate to escape. Suddenly, the privations endured over the past six years took on a different meaning. Compared to those who had been destined to remain behind in Europe and face the wrath of the Nazis, our lives seemed to have been an extended holiday in an exotic Asian city. Of the more than 18,000 Jews who had sought refuge in this strange city of Shanghai, it is estimated that fewer that 1,650 succumbed between the war's peak period of 1939 and 1945. And these deaths were more due to health reasons than political ones.

With the arrival of the American forces, life in the ghetto started to undergo dramatic changes. The speedy repatriation of the Japanese occupying troops brought some normalcy and stability into our lives. Many of the refugees with good command of the English language, as well as those with secretarial or other skills, found employment as civilian workers for the U.S. Army and other groups. Shortly after being liberated, Mama and members of the medical community in Hongkew were invited to tour a visiting American hospital ship. As refreshments were being served, she found herself in conversation with one of the ship's doctors. He told her, much to her shock and surprise, that Shanghai had been targeted for intense bombardment and that areas like Hongkew were to have been demolished. Although the Chinese had vehemently opposed this plan, they eventually gave their permission.

The orders had gone out just weeks before the August attacks on Japan, but American bombers had been prevented from accomplishing their task due to the persistent bad weather that summer.

Despite the general feeling of optimism throughout Shanghai and knowing that we were fortunate to be alive, there still remained the problem of food shortages. To compensate, we received cartons containing army rations consisting of a large can of corned beef, many smaller cans of biscuits, fruit, juices, vegetables, and candy. It was a veritable cornucopia of sustenance and eagerly welcomed by the refugees. The corned beef, however, was something of which we would quickly eat our fill. Papa, an unrepentant smoker, and who had longed for a good cigarette for many years, now found that the American brands that were surfacing all over town were very much to his taste. Like many other items, cigarettes were often bought on the burgeoning black market.

A popular destination where many children, including myself, liked to gather around this time was in front of an old five-storey office building that served as an American army barracks. We would carry on until we drew the attention of the soldiers, who would then shower us with candies, chocolate bars, and bubble gum. Everyone scrambled madly all over the sidewalk to collect the bounty. Sometimes the generous but mischievous soldiers would drop water–filled condoms, which we believed to be balloons, thoroughly drenching the candy scavengers bellow.

The planned departure of thousands of displaced persons was now underway. The quick exodus from Shanghai by the majority of the Jewish community became the most important priority. Many applied for and received visas to the United States, Brazil, and Australia; some even returned to Germany and Austria. Mama and Papa, however, decided to remain in China, if at all possible. This decision did not come as a surprise to their friends, but to many others it seemed incomprehensible that anyone would want to remain. Mama believed from day one that she was destined to be here. She and Papa had come to love the city and its people. Papa was hopeful that, with the revitalization of Shanghai, his book business would thrive. He recognized the opportunity to provide much-needed books, academic and other categories, for a growing community of foreigners and educated Chinese. His energies became focused on finding a suitable business establishment and a new home well outside the narrow confines of Hongkew. He also began to re-establish contacts with the European publishing world, with the intention of sourcing and importing books for the Chinese market. Although there was much chaos and things did not always proceed as quickly as one would like, Hongkew remained our home for some time after the end of hostilities.

One afternoon, Opa and I were lazing away the time on the docks of the Whangpoo River near the famous Bund. It was a gorgeous day. We had taken up position on a favourite bench to watch the traffic on one of the busiest rivers in all of Asia. The entire stretch of the harbour was filled with naval ships of all sizes, junks, small Chinese fishing boats, and some international shipping vessels, which had returned to Shanghai after the end of the war.

An approaching motor launch did not particularly surprise us until the craft headed directly toward us and stopped nearby. Two sailors jumped onto the dock and came over to where we were sitting. "Good afternoon, sir, young lady," said one of the sailors. "Hope you haven't been waiting too long, but as you can imagine we've been quite busy ferrying all kinds of civilians to our ship." Needless to say we did not have a clue what he was talking about. Opa gave the men a questioning glance. The other sailor, like his shipmate, believing we were civilians ready to be picked up, announced it was time for us join a number of children and adults already at the giant party on one of the British warships anchored out on the river. Though Opa was somewhat apprehensive by this sudden development, I persuaded him to go along.

Upon our arrival, we soon realized that the entire ship had been transformed into a huge playground. Balloons and streamers hung from every corner available. Games of all kinds amused the children on every deck. Slides had been built between the decks, and big armchairs attached to cannons by ropes offered dizzying rides for those children fearless enough to try them. Being the daredevil that I was, I could not get enough of the action. The ship was also awash with food and drink for everyone. It was a floating fairyland!

Opa and I eventually discovered that, technically, we should not have been there. We were picked up from the dockside by mistake. The British Navy had arranged the event for the amusement and delight of the prisoner of war camp survivors. When Opa explained the error to an officer, expecting to be whisked back ashore, the kind gentleman assured him we were more than welcome to stay and participate in the celebrations of newfound freedom. The next few hours were unforgettable. At sunset we departed once again by launch. This time we were laden with bags of candy, cookies, fresh fruit, and other goodies. When we arrived home with this bounty, Mama and Papa were delighted by our good fortune, especially Papa, who had a sweet tooth equal to mine.

Although life was changing once again for my family, technically for the better, the situation in Shanghai and the rest of China was far from stable, and nobody was sure what the future would bring. We were optimistic that it could only get better. The face of Shanghai was also undergoing a transformation. The dramatic exodus of the refugees, which transpired over a fourteen-month period or so, had marked the beginning of the end for the Jewish community. It was a process that from a trickle escalated into a flood and then back to a trickle, until only a few of the refugees remained. Many of the long-established Jewish families lingered on, but most would eventually leave as the inevitable Communist takeover of China became a reality.

Australia, the United States, and Canada were among the destinations of choice for most of those who had suffered through the war in Hongkew. Some, but not many, returned to Europe. Many others, particularly the members of the popular Betar Movement, looked towards Palestine for their new home. Members of this youthful Zionist organization would play vital roles in the struggle against the British Mandate and in the establishment of the State of Israel. The departure of the Japanese left a power vacuum that affected not just Shanghai but all those Chinese territories that had been occupied. Their departure would gradually throw the country into further chaos as the Communists, who had been on the fringes for more than twenty-five years, sought to establish themselves as China's ruling government. The dominant Nationalist Chinese party, under the leadership of Chiang Kai Shek, supported by the Americans because of their anti-Communist stance, was corrupt to the core.

During those heady post-war days in Shanghai, there was nothing that did not become available to those who could afford it. Every bureaucrat and government official could, and expected to be, bribed. Even the most unimportant and trivial application at a government office had to be accompanied by an appropriate "gift" of money known as "kumsha." Whatever commodities not available through the usual retail outlets could be found on the black market, to which officials more or less turned a blind eye. Communist victories, meanwhile, were reported from the north and west. Everyone wondered how this new drama, the clash between the Nationalists and Communists, would end.

For the next nine months, following the end of the war in Shanghai, we remained in Hongkew where our lives gradually improved. The Prokosches had left. We did not know where they went to but their bickering certainly was not missed. Yetty and her new husband emmigrated to San Francisco, a popular destination for quite a number of the now "former" refugees. Mama was sad to see Yetty go, but they would remain in touch for the rest of their lives. Papa continued the long trek to his bookstore on Avenue Joffre in the French Concession. He started putting out feelers for a new home for us. I mixed the tedium of school days with the excitement of weekends spent hanging out on the streets. Sometimes I skipped school when the mood struck me. The Shanghai I had known for nearly ten years was rapidly disappearing, but it still was anything but a boring town.

3

Shanghai 1946 - 1953

安娜樂麗

ANOTHER NEW BEGINNING

Papa, who knew Shanghai inside and out, found a new location for us to live. It was near the French Concession, which had now reverted back from French control to Chinese ownership ushering in a new era and the total demise of the foreign concessions. We were all excited about moving back to a part of the city, where we had spent a few happy years.

Sadly, our loyal cat Heika had passed away. For some reason he drank contaminated water from a dye factory run-off not far from our home on Alcock Road. Mama, always looking for the deeper meaning of things, was under the impression he did this knowingly because he sensed there was another change coming into our lives. To her, it was a cat suicide. "Think of it, he never drank from that water all the years we have been here because cats know not to drink poisoned water," she explained to us. "Poor Heika didn't want to leave here again. He drank that water on purpose knowing he would die." Unfortunately, he did not die instantly after drinking the water. To put him out of his suffering, Mama took him to a veterinarian for an injection. I was saddened by Heika's death but was promised he would be replaced by another pet.

Our new, four-storey home on Weihaiwei Road, which Papa had purchased outright instead of renting, was in a clean, pleasant neighbourhood that was part of a larger enclave of similar houses. They were built in rows off a wide, central street. Smaller laneways connected the houses together. The whole group, consisting of some fifty houses, was situated behind a wall with a wide wooden security gate. A grumpy watchman, who kept out strangers after ten o'clock at night, guarded the enclave. Shanghai, which had always had a notoriously high crime rate, was subject to even more lawlessness since the end of the war, especially with the waves of impoverished newcomers flooding to the city from other parts of China.

Your Favorite Bookstore

The Western Arts Gallery

is moving in the beginning of June

to new own premises at

904 Weihaiwei Road

(Between Seymour Road and Avenue Foch)

We sincerely hope to welcome you there very soon

Western Arts Gallery moving announcement

Before the war, the notorious Triads, who had the city in its grips, mostly controlled crime. Under Japanese rule only the activities of the Triads were tolerated. Common everyday crimes by perpetrators not under the wing of the Triads were dealt with swiftly and mercilessly. The chaos and corruption that was the norm in post-war Shanghai was an ideal climate for breaking the law. Petty crimes such as break-ins were plentiful and daily occurrences. Other than being robbed by one of our hired help, which we only discovered after some time had lapsed, we were not victimized by the chaos.

In June 1946, we eagerly moved into our new residence. It had been nearly a year since the war had ended, and we were happy to be out of Hongkew at last. Although quite compact, the building could not have been more ideal. Not only did it have spacious living quarters, the street level area, which had previously been a bar, was perfect for Papa's book business. The frontage had two large display windows, which at the end of each business day were covered up by wooden slats. This precaution was to keep the glass safe from vandals and to deter robbers from entering the premises.

Papa had become the sole proprietor of the Western Arts Gallery, having bought out Kurt Schwartz. His former business partner had applied for immigration papers to the United States. The Weihaiwei Road location of the Western Arts Gallery was the first shop Papa could truly call his own since the expropriation of Oliva Buchhandlung in Berlin. It was hard to believe that more than ten years had gone by since those days under the Nazis. Life was good now, and Papa could not have been happier with the new arrangement because he no longer had to leave home to make a living. After the long hours he used to spend away from us in Hongkew, having him close by all the time was a real treat.

Our living space was located on the four floors above the store. Stairs from the ground floor led up to a large kitchen. A short flight of steps led to a living-dining room and an adjacent bathroom. The third floor had a room that was occupied by Opa. The master bedroom, located on the fourth floor, was under the eaves of the house and was quite large. Despite the regal improvements of this new place in comparison to our cramped, single room in Hongkew, some important amenities were still lacking. Even though equipped with a flush toilet, our new home had no hot running water. It was necessary to order heated water ahead of time from commercially run "hot water shops" in the neighbourhood. There was one down the street from us, and our daily supply was delivered in buckets suspended from bamboo poles that were carried by one or two persons. This was a time-consuming and sometimes expensive process. Central heating was also lacking. During the frigid winters the living-dining room was heated with a wood-burning stove. When in use for cooking, the kitchen stove was the only source of warmth in that room. The bedrooms were not heated and were very unpleasant during the winter. Hot water bottles were used to warm the beds; flannel pyjamas were a must. Small electric heaters, which barely kept out the cold, heated the bookshop.

Once again, the object of my desire, a room of my own, did not materialize. I was deeply disappointed. Now that I was ten-years-old, I was beginning to feel a need for my own private space. Off to one side of the master bedroom was an alcove, no larger than a walk-in closet. The original owners had intended to use it as a small bathroom. This cramped space was assigned to me as sleeping quarters. It had barely enough room for my bed; my belongings were piled on a single shelf above the bed.

When the door was closed it felt like a tomb; fortunately it had a small window. The older I got, the more I resented being stuck in this alcove. I felt like I was little more than a guest in my parents' bedroom. Other than providing the basics like shelter, food, clothing, and an education, Mama and Papa were not particularly sensitive to the needs of a child approaching adolescence.

After moving to Weihaiwei Road, Mama and Papa's social life became more front and centre. It was as if they were reliving their Berlin days when newlyweds. The lack of concern Mama and Papa showed for me at this stage of my life only made me more rebellious and independent. In general, however, my life started taking on different and much more exciting proportions now. To some degree, this made up for the lack of my own room.

The prospects of a new school, discoveries, adventures, and friends made small discomforts quite bearable. Like the old Western Arts Gallery, the new one quickly became one of my favourite places to be. I, too, had become an avid reader, and the many varied books offered me solace and escape: they abetted my flights of fantasy. Now that Papa was close by, I spent as much time with him as possible to make up for the many years of the twelve to fourteen hour days he was away from home. Although there were a number of other antiquarian bookshops in town, Papa's store enjoyed great popularity. Like the previous location on Avenue Joffre, it was a meeting place for book lovers and intellectuals. They not only spent time in the store but also were often invited upstairs for afternoon coffee and cake around the trusty old oak dining room table from Berlin. Around this table, which seated twelve, everything was discussed: what the future could possibly hold for us in Shanghai, the Communists vs. the Nationalists, the tragedy that befell the Jews in Europe, and the diverse subjects that were of interest to Papa and Mama and their like-minded friends. These discussions did not hold much interest for me, but fortunately there was some idle gossip and stories of personal adventures and exploits that did pique my curiosity.

A gathering of like-minded friends

At one time the entire area on Weihaiwei Road had been a very large piece of land belonging to the wealthy Hardoun family. Their huge holdings were gradually sold off and developed into commercial properties and dwellings like the one we now occupied. The family had retained a large walled-in property that was inaccessible to the general public. I, however, eventually gained entry by befriending a young member of the reclusive Hardoun family. The Hardouns had settled in Shanghai as part of the original Iraqi Sephardic community. Included in that illustrious company were the Sassoons and Kadoories, with whom the Hardouns had done so much to alleviate the suffering of the Jewish refugees. In his later years, the current patriarch of the Hardoun family married a Chinese lady who had been a servant in his employ. They were childless but had adopted a number of young children of many nationalities and raised them in their opulent house. It was one of these adopted children, Emily Hardoun, whom I befriended. Emily was much older than I, somewhere in her twenties, and I came to regard her more as an older sister than just a friend.

One day, as I stood at the gate of the property and tried to figure a way to sneak in, I encountered Emily. She eyed me with a certain air of suspicion but she seemed friendly enough. "Hello there. What are you up to? You realize this is private property, don't you?" Emily said, knowing quite well my intentions to trespass. I gave her my most demure look and replied, "Nothing. Just looking. But could I please play in the garden. It looks so pretty, and I really don't have anywhere else to play except on the street. Is it okay if I come inside?" I queried. Although she was a bit apprehensive at first, she agreed to accommodate me. As usual, my disarming smile and incredible story of how I had come to live in Shanghai did not fail me. I was grateful to Emily for opening up the fairytale world that she called home. That summer I spent many happy hours there.

In the middle of a raucous and crowded city of more than four million souls, there existed this huge garden gone completely wild. It was a veritable jungle overgrown with tropical plants and exotic flowers. The only thing missing were elephants, tigers, and other jungle beasts. Paths, now barely visible, led to a big lake on which sat a stone boat surrounded by floating islands of flowering lotus. There was also a splendid Buddhist temple, although I do not know if anybody ever used it. Despite the neglect, the property was stunningly beautiful and I was glad to have gained entry. Buzzing insects were the only sounds to be heard; none of the noises from outside penetrated into this oasis. For me, the Hardoun compound surpassed anything I had encountered in Shanghai so far. Here, away from the trials and tribulations of everyday life, I felt like a queen of a fairy empire.

Hannelore, Stephen, and Tanya Hamburger in the Hardoun garden

Before long, the carefree summer of 1946 slipped away and reality intruded upon my dream world; I was enrolled in the Shanghai Jewish School, a renowned educational institution run by the Sephardic Jewish Community. This modern and well-appointed school was located on Seymour Road, not too far from our new home. Just before the beginning of the school year, I took the twenty-minute walk there to satisfy my curiosity. The school was built on two levels and had a central courtyard. There were separate large, well-equipped classrooms for each grade. The building was surrounded by playing fields and a sports facility. On the same grounds was a fine synagogue.

The door to the school was unlocked, and I did not hesitate to enter and wander around as if I owned the place. I found an elderly gentleman behind a desk, shuffling some paper. He looked quite dignified, tall, a bit on the thin side, and immaculately dressed in suit and tie. Although I interrupted his work he did not seem annoyed with my intrusion. "Can I help you young lady? I'm Mr. Holland, the headmaster here. And you are...?" I told him my name and explained that I had been enrolled in the school and came to explore so I would be familiar with the place when school started at the end of summer. "Well, is that so? I wish all of our new students were that enthusiastic about their studies," he quipped. I did not tell him that I was not really interested in studies so much, just the school. We had a friendly chat and I discovered he was acquainted with Papa's bookstore, which he praised as one of the best of its kind in the city. It was always nice to hear things like that. But I knew Papa ran not just one of the best, he ran the best bookstore in all of China. Of course, that was my modest opinion!

Later on, I was a bit surprised that Mr. Holland was Anglican and not Jewish. During the school year, I noticed that he always wore a yarmulke at assemblies and religious occasions. "It's been nice chatting with you, Hannelore, but you will have to excuse me now. I have quite a bit of work to do with school starting up shortly. Give my regards to your father," he finally said, letting me know I should be on my way. I said goodbye and left quite pleased with the prospect of attending this school. I surprised myself by admitting I was looking forward to going to school, when up to then I had only looked forward to going home from such establishments.

After years of makeshift schools, the Shanghai Jewish School became the first "real" school I attended. I was impressed by what an actual school entailed and, for the first time in my life as a student, I did not put up a fuss about having to get an education. The curriculum at the Shanghai Jewish School was based on the British school system and I began my sojourn there in the Upper Second form. Classes were divided into Lower and Upper forms, with the Upper Sixth being the graduating year. The teaching staff was comprised of both men and women, clearly hired for their experience and expertise in their subject areas. Hebrew classes and Old Testament Bible studies were mandatory, as well as the usual subjects such as math and science. Great emphasis was placed on participating in competitive sports; much time was spent in training for the annual sports days. Although I did not care much for sports, my thin wiry legs were ideal for the "long jump" and I won some ribbons in that event. My year at the school was by and large quite happy and, though I was never at the top of my class, I managed to pass all the subjects. I never really gave much thought to the personal sacrifices my parents had to make in order to send me. The difficulty of raising money to cover the fees became obvious when I had to be taken out of school after my fist year and was provided with a tutor.

During the year I was not attending the Shanghai Jewish School, I helped out at the Wonderland Kindergarten. Anna Marie Pordes and Martha Schwartz ran it. Mrs. Schwartz was the wife of Papa's former business partner. I was eleven years old, and the confidence placed in me by the adult world greatly reinforced my self-esteem. It was my job to play games with the dozen or so little ones entrusted into my care. I also helped with serving lunch and cleaning-up after the children had left for the day. I, then, returned home for a session with my tutor, an elderly German lady who did her best to make sure I did not fall too far behind in my studies. I do believe that I managed to learn much more from the many books I read in Papa's store and the dinner table conversations I was privy to than from that well-intentioned lady.

Not too long after I started helping out at the kindergarten, Martha and Kurt Schwartz announced they were leaving Shanghai. Their immigration papers had finally been processed, and they were moving to San Francisco. Like many of the friendships my family formed in Shanghai, this one would also remain intact. After the many years as Papa's partner, Mr. Schwartz had inherited a genuine passion for the book business. Upon his arrival in

San Francisco, he opened a store of his own. It soon became a successful business venture and he eventually passed the store on to his son.

Spring of 1947 saw the arrival of my baby brother, Stephen. He was a month late and weighed in at 11 pounds. Though Mama and Papa had not planned for another child, he was a welcome addition to the family and much loved. Opa, of course, was delighted with his new grandson. Due to the restrictions of sleeping space, Stephen's crib was put at the end of our parents' bed, where it remained for the duration of our occupation of the house. It was a large crib and had to serve him for six years. I loved my little brother, but his crying in the middle of the night was something that took time to get used to.

In the oppressive summer heat of August 1947, I was sent to spend two weeks with friends in the country. This little vacation away from home had a twofold purpose: Mama and Papa believed it was a nice change for me, and because Mama needed the rest. The heat and humidity, as usual, did not agree with her. Those two weeks, despite the sincere efforts of my hosts and their three children to keep me amused, bored me to tears and were fraught with various degrees of peril. Toilet facilities consisted of a large and deep trench located some distance from the house and was filled daily with quicklime to absorb the contents. One stood or squatted at the edge of a steep, slippery slope and aimed in the general direction of the hole. This feat was treacherous enough during daylight hours, but I lived in fear of having to negotiate my way there at night with the ever-present danger of possibly falling in, not to mention the critters that were roaming around. I loved adventure and risk but I was a city adventurer, not the country type. I was relieved to go home again to my friends, the small modern conveniences of the city, and the kind of situations to which I was a little more accustomed.

Life in Shanghai during the post-war years took on a frenetic quality for my parents and their friends. It was as if everyone needed to make up for the privations and lost years of the terrible war. Evenings spent at home as a family became a rare occurrence. Mama and Papa seemed like they were on some kind of mission to recapture their halcyon nightlife days in pre-war Berlin. They met their friends in nightclubs, coffee houses, and casinos. Quite often, Shanghai church groups ran these casinos as fundraising enterprises. Although Papa did not care much for games of chance, the roulette wheel enchanted him. Mama revelled in games that required a bit of intellect. She avoided the slots and roulette, choosing instead to focus on card games like poker, chemin de fer, baccarat, and blackjack. She was an excellent card player; and much to Papa's delight she usually won more money than she lost. One of the more opulent gaming clubs allowed the winning gamblers a half-hour lead time to get away safely with their largesse before permitting any one else to leave, providing them with a chauffeur-driven limousine. These precautions helped ensure that the lucky gamblers would not be victimized by the less fortunate fans of games of chance or by opportunistic robbers lurking nearby. To the best of my knowledge, no one was ever robbed; although, I would think that resourceful bandits of the street had become aware of this ploy and accosted those seen leaving early to relieve them of their winnings.

One popular gambling venue was the former Shanghai racetrack. Before the war, it was known all over Asia for its greyhound and horse races. Now it was used to house U.S. Army personnel. This changeover was a boon to the casinos, which were more than happy to accommodate the gamblers and relieve them of their cash. The Americans, in turn, put the infield to good use by converting it into a baseball diamond. They introduced children like myself to the excitement of their country's national sport. Often, on weekends, my friends and I attended these games and cheered for our favourite teams. Mama and Papa, however, had no interest in sports. They especially did not care for baseball, which was totally un-European.

There was a note of sadness to the story of the former racetrack. Immediately after the war, stray greyhounds were seen on the streets of the city where they had been abandoned after the track closed. The streets abounded with stray animals, both cats and dogs, who managed to scrounge enough scraps of food to survive. The sleek and handsome greyhounds, once pampered for the enjoyment of humans, were unable to fend for themselves. Most died of neglect and starvation. The Chinese, it seemed, had little regard for animals that competed with them for food and shelter. They had been known to make a meal out of a dog or cat. Birds and crickets, on the other hand, were caught and caged to make popular pets. On hot summer nights, the incessant chirping of the crickets in their cages while their owners sat or slept on the sidewalks gave one the feeling of being serenaded by the myriad insects of a jungle.

My dog, Tommy

I, on the other hand, acquired a mongrel dog named Tommy. I was thrilled because he was the first dog, or pet even, that I could truly call my own. He was a most welcome replacement for poor Heika. Sometimes Tommy and I serenaded the neighbours; we were a peculiar musical duo that I'm sure they would have gladly done without. Whenever I played my harmonica, at which I had become quite proficient, Tommy incessantly howled along. I'm not sure if he was actually doing this to contribute to the music or because I drove him crazy with my playing. Tommy and I became almost inseparable; he accompanied me just about everywhere I went. One day, while walking on the sidewalk adjacent to the lengthy wall surrounding the

Hardoun family compound, Tommy ran into the path of a speeding ambulance. To my horror, he was so badly hurt that Papa had to take him to the vet to be put down. I was shattered by this loving dog's death. Even though I was promised another one, I refused to have him replaced. No other dog could ever take Tommy's place. Instead, our family was given a Siamese cat by friends who were departing from Shanghai. Her name was Coffee and, like Heika before her, she was a fierce hunter.

On some of the nights that Mama and Papa were not at home, I waited for Opa to retire; then I snuck out of the house to explore the neighbourhood. Despite the dangers and hustle and bustle of the city, it was quite safe to be out at night as a foreigner in Shanghai. Just like in pre-war and wartime Shanghai, no Chinese would ever molest a young white child. But I was not overly concerned about my safety because, like all kids, I believed myself to be invincible. I thrived on doing things I was not supposed to do.

On one of my nocturnal wanderings I discovered a band of likeable families who were Portuguese Gypsies. I was immediately made to feel welcome by them and, in a way, I felt we were kindred spirits. This was not just because of my wanderlust but because their people also had been persecuted by the Nazis, and many of them had died in the horrible extermination camps. My new friends resided in a number of windowless concrete structures that had once served as storage facilities for bulk goods such as aggregates and coal. These structures were open at the front and had no doors; this construction had been to facilitate easy access for dump trucks and bulldozers. The gypsies covered these gaping entrances with ragged tarps. Although the storage units provided shelter from rain and snow, it was a terrible place to be, especially during the frigid winter months. Each of the units was heated with scraps of wood burned in old oil drums. These drums were cut open at the top and had some holes punched in the sides to provide a draft to feed the flames. Furthermore, the locale of these concrete structures was equally gloomy, barren, and totally devoid of trees, grass, or even weeds.

The lust for life these nearly homeless people exhibited belied the wretched surroundings they inhabited. I was very much attracted to them and found them truly fascinating. Their dark olive complexions, long jet-black hair, and brightly coloured dress captured my imagination and further stirred up my already adventurous nature. What I truly found disarming was that they were always cheerful despite the dire conditions in which they lived. Their passion for life was infectious; the stories of their nomadic lives and escapades were riveting. Nearly everyone seemed to be able to play all sorts of musical instruments. Fiery flamenco music and exotic dancing was always the highlight of an evening. Though Mama and Papa would not have approved of these friends, I spent many enthralling and carefree hours with the gypsies.

Quite often I lost all track of time, becoming totally absorbed in the moment because that is how the gypsies lived: in the "here and now", no past no future. When someone reminded me that it was time to go, I quickly took my leave and rushed home. I leapt up the steps to my alcove like a nimble cat so I would not wake Opa. Then I jumped fully clothed into bed, arriving just moments before my unsuspecting parents came home. I liked to think I was fooling them; if they did have an inkling of my nocturnal activities, they never confronted me about them.

On most nights when Mama and Papa were out, I would stay home and amuse myself in various ways. I was a voracious reader and there certainly were enough books at hand to keep me occupied. We had a fairly extensive record collection and a wind-up gramophone on which to play them. I enjoyed listening to all kinds of music, but my favourite was German tenor Richard Tauber. From our living room window I liked watching bats fly around, illuminated by the street lights directly in front of our building. On cloudless full-moon nights, I loved to go into the Hardoun gardens and train Papa's binoculars on the glowing disk in the sky. The gardens were an ideal place to view the moon, which looked humongous and revealed all its craters through the binoculars.

In addition to Emily Hardoun and the gypsies, I also started making Chinese friends of my own age, something I had not really had the opportunity to do in the French Concession and Hongkew. Although never fluent in Chinese, my ability to communicate in this difficult language improved greatly after moving to Weihaiwei Road. I became close friends with the Yang family, who lived just down the street from me, and their home became my home away from home. They had six children ranging in age from five to seventeen with whom I became very close. On many occasions I ate meals with the Yangs, and they introduced me to all kinds of delicious Chinese dishes. I was not familiar with these because the only indigenous foods I really knew were the snack variety sold by street vendors. The Yangs were a musical family and owned an ornate pump organ that they sometimes allowed me to play. To their and my surprise, I was able to pick out simple tunes on this wonderful instrument. Mr.Yang, like many Shanghailanders, had adopted western traits from years of being exposed to the foreign community. He liked playing western tunes on the organ and, much to his delight, I knew the words to some of his favourite songs in the original English or German.

Over the years, I had become used to the hordes of beggars who were very much a part of the city tapestry. They were considerably worse off than my gypsy friends and were in such overwhelming numbers. One could not begin to be of help to them, especially as a penniless child such as myself. Like most of the more favoured residents of the city I had learned to walk by and ignore the ragged, often maimed, individuals of all ages who lay or sat on the sidewalks of every street, hands outstretched for help. On bitterly cold winter mornings, it was not unusual to find the frozen body of someone who had been unable to find shelter. Despite better times having arrived in Shanghai since the end of the war, there seemed to be more beggars populating the streets. No doubt, this could be attributed to the influx of people from the countryside who came looking for a better life. In many cases what they found was worse than what they had left behind. Papa, ever the one to care about the plight of others, started a little Saturday morning ritual that saw him give a few pennies each to the half dozen beggars who congregated in front of the store.

Since the end of the war, the sidewalks had seen an increase in the number of vendors with portable kitchens and wagons offering all kinds of dried fruits and sweetmeats. In spring, sweet yams heated in portable clay ovens then dabbed in hot pepper sauce were my favourite; in fall, I indulged in hot chestnuts. Then there were puffed rice cakes, candied grapes, crab apples, and peanut candy. These were my childhood delights. With so much food, inexpensive and readily available, anyone with a bit of change in their pockets could have a veritable outdoor feast any day of the week. How different those times were from just a few years earlier when any kind of sustenance was scarce. Being the food lover I was, I partook in all the delicacies offered on the street. I should have been sick most of the time with various intestinal ailments, but I managed to take it all in without ill effect. Even though I had developed some immunity to the risky food found on the streets, it remained dangerous to eat any fresh vegetables or to drink water that had not been boiled. Insects of all kinds, especially cockroaches, remained endemic. Keeping them out of one's food was a daily challenge, no matter how hygienic the environment or what extreme measures were taken to keep them at bay.

During these better times and more relaxed social gatherings, Mama had been invited to a very elegant tea party. It happened to be held by a particularly fussy friend, who ran her kitchen as if she were an army sergeant. There, Mama had an encounter of the insect kind. While sipping on a very good cup of coffee and enjoying a piece of cake, she was startled by something crunchy in her mouth. She took out her handkerchief and, as delicately as possible, removed the intruder from her mouth. She was not at all surprised that the unwanted ingredient was a roach! Mama diplomatically displayed no shock and did not raise an issue with her friend, who would have been greatly mortified and embarrassed. This friend believed that insects were a problem faced by the rest of the city and not by her.

Food stories abounded and were a constant source of amusement, although in many cases were enough to sicken even the least squeamish. A favourite story that made the rounds regarded an impeccable and well-known society hostess whose delicious toasted sandwiches were the rave of the city. Her Chinese cook, who prepared these mouth-watering titbits, was famous far and wide, making the hostess the envy of her friends. After several very successful afternoon teas, the society matron was persuaded by her guests to let them in on her cook's secret. The secret had never been revealed. When they arrived in the kitchen they were just in time to observe the cook lining up several slices of bread upon which he bestowed a thin spray of water directly out of his mouth. After a moment of shocked silence, the guests departed, and the reputation of the lady became, as one might say, "toast"!

* * *

The escalating success of Papa's bookshop encouraged him to consider expansion. After doing some research, he decided to open small branch stores in Nanking and Peking. He stocked these stores with just enough inventory to establish a presence and attract a customer base. To supplement the books in stock, he supplied his employees with detailed, regularly updated catalogues listing the rare books he stocked in the Shanghai store or those he was able to obtain from his many sources. His new connections in Europe were now valuable suppliers of recently published scientific and medical books sought after by university libraries, professionals, and well-to-do students. Papa had acquired an importing license after paying the usual bribes that accompanied all bureaucratic transactions. He was kept busy importing and distributing textbooks, art, and library books in addition to the hard-to-find collector's books for which all three locations of the Western Arts Gallery were now renowned.

Papa and Mama regularly went to Peking and Nanking for short visits to look after his thriving business interests. I took advantage of these absences to skip school and indulge in a favourite new pastime–sneaking into a local cinema, The Uptown Theatre. The theatre was located at the rear of a shopping arcade and had its main entrance there. At the back, adjacent to a laneway, was the rear exit. Most patrons used it to leave the theatre. This was my point of entry. Despite my age, I was still quite small and had honed my skills of sneaking into the theatre into a fine art. I was so good at slipping through the exiting bodies that I never once got caught and got to see all the latest movies for free. The theatre played mostly American movies, which I had become a big fan. My love affair with the cinema led me to take up a new hobby: perusing magazines for pictures of my favourite movie stars, cutting them out, and pasting them in to a scrapbook. Around this time I also became an avid collector of comic books such as *Captain Marvel, The Green Hornet,* and *Terry and the*

Pirates. I had easy access to these books, as they were some of the items Papa imported. They were a surprisingly big hit with many of his less serious readers. Over the years I acquired a collection that numbered in the hundreds.

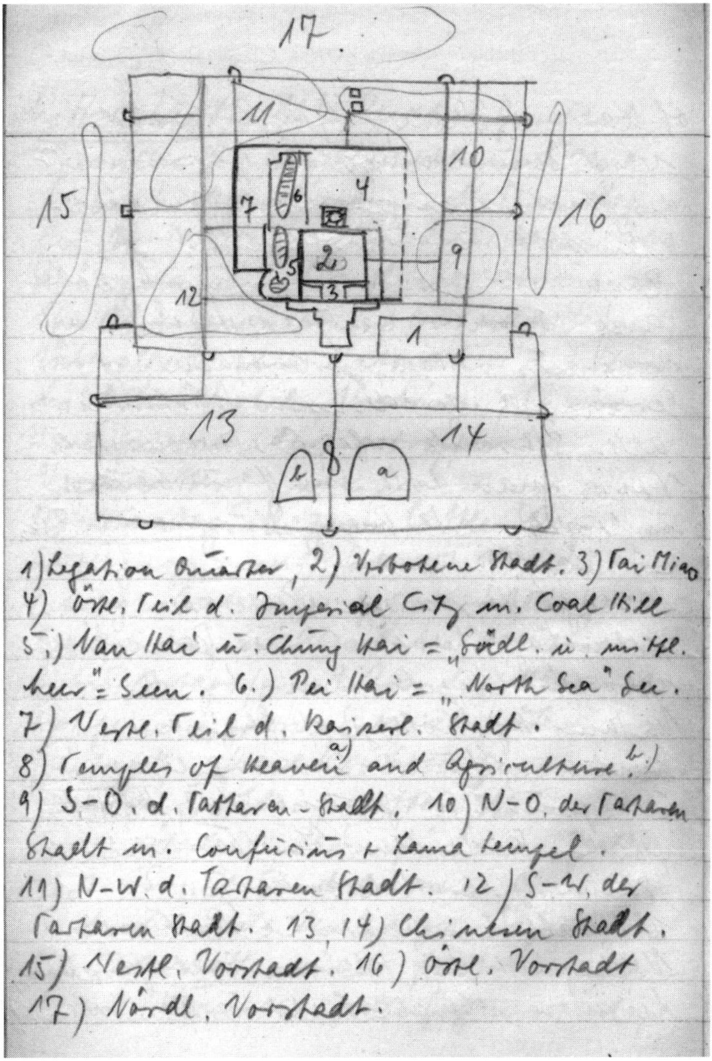

Mama's travel notes from Peking, April 12, 1948

安娜樂麗

A NEW MENACE APPROACHES

Though the hectic city life of Shanghai appeared to continue unhindered on a daily basis, some disquieting news was circulating among the citizens of the foreign community. In the far north of the country, a rag-tag army of wartime Communist partisans, who had successfully managed to harass the Japanese throughout the war years, were preparing to arm and march towards the south. Under the charismatic and determined leadership of Mao Tse Tung, the Communist forces, who had been driven underground by the Nationalist Armies of Chang Kai Shek in the 1920s, were now preparing to make their move. With a few captured Japanese arms and some help from the USSR, the Communists were beginning to capture more and more villages and towns, recruiting and adding to their army a large number of eager young men willing to fight for the cause.

While the citizens of the larger and more industrialized cities of the south perceived themselves to be in little danger, foreigners and foreign-run businesses and financial institutions felt uneasy enough to plan their eventual departure. It was believed that it would only be a matter of time before China joined Russia as a major Communist ruled nation. Foo Dor, the young Chinese man Mama and Papa had taken on to help around the house, told stories of the appalling living conditions of his family and most villagers and farm peasants in the countryside. It came as no surprise, he mentioned, that the oppressed masses were welcoming the Liberation Armies with open arms and little opposition. Daily, the conditions under the Nationalists worsened. Even in the big cities, the financial situation was deteriorating. Nationalist leaders, already wealthy from years of corrupt practices, horded an even larger fortune for a new life after their glory days came to an end–something they knew was at hand. Amidst all the rumours of impending doom, Mama and Papa remained optimistic about their future in Shanghai and decided to stay on. Moreover, most people felt safe and life on the whole proceeded normally, even for my family and me. But the eventual outcome of the political dramas being played out in many parts of China would be another reality check for us. It is ironic that Mama and Papa, who had been so intuitive regarding the threat of the Nazis a decade earlier, had adopted the same ill-perceived attitude that had led so many fellow Jews to remain in Germany.

The summer of 1948 brought with it a personal crisis for our household. Opa complained of not feeling well and was the victim of fainting spells. He was hospitalised and diagnosed with Hodgkin's Disease, a form of leukaemia for which there was no cure. The thought of losing my beloved grandfather weighed heavily on my mind.

We prepared ourselves for the worst. At the beginning of the new school year, with enough money scraped together by Papa for tuition, I reluctantly returned to the Shanghai Jewish School. I had become used to my German tutor's informal method of lessons, which could

Opa, 1948

Hannelore, 1948

be given either at home, in a park, or at the Lutheran Church. To be reintroduced to the rigours of a structured curriculum held little interest for me. I resumed my studies in a new and higher grade and had no trouble with the curriculum. My tutor had done an excellent job during the past year keeping me on a parallel course with the studies received by my peers.

I belonged to a class of fifteen students, among which were the children of some very well-to-do families. A student's popularity among fellow classmates often depended upon their ability to buy expensive lunches for themselves and their friends; parties were another popular social activity. A membership in one of Shanghai's exclusive private clubs was almost mandatory for success so you could invite friends for swimming and lunch parties. I was definitely not a member of the rich and infamous, nor was I too concerned about my popularity factor.

Despite not belonging to the in-crowd, I was occasionally asked to share an ordered-in lunch at school or received an invitation to swim and dine at the swank French Club. On those occasions I was always made to feel that I was the lucky recipient of a compassionate and kind act of charity. To be polite, I went through the motions of being impressed and grateful; but I felt the exact opposite for the spoiled snobs who were my benefactors. I felt much more in my element chumming around with downtrodden Chinese kids or sitting around a campfire with my gypsy friends.

In warm and sunny weather, my walk to school often took me past a vendor of a particularly tasty form of Chinese tortilla. Combined with a rolled up, deep-fried bread stick, the tortilla made a delicious adjunct to breakfast. This delicacy made many a walk to school more enjoyable. In cold and rainy weather, Papa provided transportation to school in the form of a hired pedicab. This vehicle was a large form of tricycle. It had a seat for holding two passengers between the two rear wheels. The driver energetically pedalled while seated behind the front wheel. When it rained, passengers sat beneath a covering canopy with a waterproof sheet fastened to the front to keep from being drenched. As each pedicab driver was an independent businessman, payment for every trip had to be negotiated at the start of the journey. It varied almost every time.

In the school system at that time, some students in the higher grades were selected to become prefects, and I was one of those asked to take on the task. My stint helping out at the Wonderland kindergarten had made me an ideal candidate for this position. The job of prefect was preferential and considered a privilege. I accepted it with pride and took on the responsibility of looking after a class of younger children. When the entire student body assembled before the start of classes each school day, my first duty was to make sure the children were properly lined up. This procedure was usually done in the playground, but in bad weather everyone gathered in the large assembly hall. Then, in an orderly fashion, I conducted my charges to their classroom, took roll call, and made sure everyone was seated and quiet for when the teacher entered. This being done, I quickly proceeded to my own classroom. I did find this part of my school day enjoyable enough, and it provided me with some incentive to show up, at least most of the time. The after-hours sports practices were still not a favourite activity. An indication of how badly I did at field hockey, and sports in general, were the scars I incurred that would remain with me the rest of my life.

After a few months I had resigned myself to the fact that I needed to make the best of being back in school. Other than skipping classes now and then, I was well behaved. As before, I got along well with the headmaster, Mr. Holland. In fact, as a sort of mediator, I sometimes pleaded the case for fellow students who got into trouble. This initiative scored me points with my peers, even though I was mostly unsuccessful in my defence tactics. Mr. Holland indulged my good intentions, but he never showed any favouritism. He was a righteous man who treated everyone alike.

As if the impending death of Opa was not stressful enough on us, the shadow of the Communist insurgents kept spreading across China and making its way to Peking, the nation's capital. Everyone knew it would not stop there but continue south towards Shanghai. Given the uncertainty of the times, Papa had already closed his branch operation in Nanking. He decided to make one last short journey to Peking to ascertain whether to maintain the store there. He felt that I should accompany him on this trip in order to introduce me to some of the remaining glories of this ancient city and to help take my mind off Opa's suffering. "It will be a wonderful opportunity for you to experience the nearly unchanged history of this ancient city," he said. I was reluctant to accompany him because I wanted to stay as close to Opa as possible. Papa told me there was nothing I could really do and added that this trip would probably be my only chance to go to Peking. Mama assured me that she would spend as much time with Opa as possible. I agreed to take the trip. The fact that I got a reprieve from attending school helped facilitate my decision.

Our three-hour flight to Peking was rough and anxiety-ridden. The ancient propeller-driven plane was small and, like so much of the mechanical equipment in China at that time, far from being in the best shape. We arrived on a crisp, late September afternoon and were met at the airport by the family who had been looking after the Peking store. They had invited us to be their guests in their spacious quarters, located in what was called the Foreign Legation. This residential area of western-style homes was almost exclusively reserved for the members of the foreign community: diplomats, business people, and teachers. In sharp contrast to Shanghai, most of the Chinese dwellings in Peking were one-storey structures built around courtyards. These were built behind walls accessible only by gates, either guarded or locked, and located in small laneways called "Hutungs." The number of courtyards and the opulence of the adjacent buildings determined the wealth and status of the owners of these properties. The city was almost completely occupied by such one-storey homes, the exception being the Wagons-Lits Hotel, which boasted some six storeys and claimed the distinction of being Peking's highest western-style structure.

One of the many sights and sounds that reminded me of the close proximity of the desert and of the age of the city was the use of camels for the delivery of coal and other daily needs of the residents. I was told that the nearness of the Gobi Desert was even more obvious in spring, when Peking was battered by a number of sandstorms that left behind a layer of sand on everything. Whereas Shanghai tended to impress upon first-time visitors a feeling of chaos and frenetic disharmony, Peking instilled a sense of awe and near-serenity.

Since arriving in China in 1939, this was my first epic sojourn outside of Shanghai. I was glad I had decided to accompany Papa after all, although I did have second thoughts on the wild airplane ride. Papa was able to wrap up the business end of his trip in very short order; he reluctantly decided to liquidate the stock of the Peking store because he feared all would be lost when the Communists took over. Having to give up yet another venture that he had worked so hard to establish saddened him, but he was buoyed by the prospect of taking me on a discovery tour of the city. Papa had never been one to let negative things get him down for long and was quite adept at making the best of a bad situation. I could not wait to feast my eyes on the sights Papa had told me so much about, especially the Forbidden City.

Within the walled city of Peking, at one end of Tiananmen Square, was the walled city that was home to twenty-four Ming and Ch'ing emperors: the fabled Forbidden City. Papa was most excited to be here with me and gave me a first-hand account of how this mind-boggling place came into existence. He knew he could never bore me with facts and dates pertaining to antiquity. Like him, I had an insatiable appetite for what came before us. "The Forbidden City was ordered in the early 1400s by the Ming emperors and was constructed in an amazingly short period of fifteen years," he began to tell me with the authority of a college professor. I knew that he was aware of the exact dates of everything but, not to make it too formal, he generalized. "The Ming Emperors took control of China in 1368 after the Mongolian Yuan Dynasty. The famous Kublai Khan had founded this Dynasty in the late 1200s. You may remember Kublai Khan as the emperor who received Marco Polo." I nodded in agreement and he continued with the little history lesson. "The Ming's rule lasted quite a bit longer than the Yuan and didn't come to an end until the mid-1600s. That's when the Manchurian Ch'ing family overthrew them. The Ch'ings were the last of the great dynasties and survived until not that long ago, 1911 to be exact. The last emperor, P'u Yi, was only five-years-old when China's royalty came to an end."

"A five-year-old emperor, wow!" I blurted out. "Now that's something I could have gotten into, Papa. Empress Hannelore of China. It has a nice ring to it, don't you think?" He chuckled at my delusions of grandeur and reminded me that when I was that age, I might as well have been the empress of Hongkew. "The way you cavorted around the place, it was as if you owned it," he jibed. I was impressed by Papa's account of the origin of the Forbidden City but not nearly as much as by the reality of what lay before us. The approaches to the gates of this royal domain were roads epic in scale. Later I was told they were many times the width of the Champs Elysees in Paris. It was a truly staggering sight. We came to the colossal Meridian Gate, the main entrance to the 250 acre domain, which was flanked by imposing 35 foot high vermillion coloured perimeter walls. For countless generations, only members of the royal families, privileged Chinese nobles, high-raking court officials, and court favourites were permitted to enter. Only occasional intrusions by a few invited diplomats and foreign visitors of state were tolerated.

I truly felt privileged to walk through this gate and imagined that I was on a mission of diplomatic importance. Although many parts of the Forbidden City were no longer off limits to the many tourists who flocked there, much was still inaccessible. The public could only visit a fine museum, courtyards, beautiful gardens, and a number of throne rooms, with their rich furnishings and displays of gifts left for the emperors by foreign dignitaries. A large part of the private quarters, at one time occupied by former court members and the emperors' families, were still out of bounds. Everywhere I looked were scenes of splendour and opulence that made unforgettable impressions on my eyes and on my mind. Red was the dominant colour, followed by yellow. Papa explained that red was the symbolic colour of imperial power. He told me the compound had a total of 9,999 rooms. This number was significant because nine was the lucky number of the royal families. Most breath-taking were the golden ceramic tiles that adorned all the roofs of this ancient palace. The contrast between the bright golden roofs and the unpolluted clear blue skies of Peking to the industrial miasma of Shanghai was startling. Still within the confines of the city, high on a hillside, stood the Winter Palace. Its splendid white-domed roof glittered in the bright autumn sunlight; and, below, a gentle wind stirred the rippling waters of an artificial lake. The lake had become a favourite playground for the citizens of Peking.

Peking, 1948

Our next destination was the Summer Palace, with its spectacular gardens, lakes, and buildings nestled among the trees of the countryside, some miles outside of the city.

Peking, 1948

As we walked through the stately painted hallways of this magnificent place, we were overwhelmed by the sheer lavishness, wealth, and imagination that went into the building of these pleasure domes. Out on the luxuriant grounds, a marble boat, permanently moored on the large artificial lake, boggled my imagination. At one time, this seemingly unfloatable boat was propelled around the lake by the backbreaking efforts of slaves. It was the tea pavilion of the late Empress Dowager and her guests. To my surprise I realized that the boat on the Hardoun property was a replica of the boat on this lake.

Another place of enchantment was one of the world's great architectural wonders, the Temple of Heaven. With its perfectly round blue-tiled roof, it sat in harmonious placement on the surrounding marble terraces, built one on top of another. When one stood in a certain place and whispered, the wonder of acoustical engineering returned and amplified the whisper many times over. Papa, who had studiously acquainted himself with the history of all these places, made the perfect guide: he shared fascinating nuggets of information to teach and amuse me. This adventure sure beat going to school, although, technically, it could have been considered an educational field trip.

After exploring the more opulent settings of Peking we ventured to some of the more common but equally fascinating destinations. One of these was the city's famous outdoor Thieves Market, which was on Papa's well-planned itinerary. If one happened to be the hapless victim of a robbery in Peking, with any luck and for a price, the stolen items could be repossessed at this market the next day. No questions asked, no accusations made, and no police raids: this was China. Fortunately, we did not have anything stolen. The visit to the Thieves Market was simply for curiosity's sake and to look for a bargain or two.

At the market were vendors selling every known imaginable object. As loudly as possible, they shouted out the attractions of their wares to the crowds walking by. We bought a quaint silver bracelet for Mama that the vendor purported to be an antique, but Papa knew it to be a cleverly aged reproduction. He did not accuse the vendor of being deceitful because that would have been very impolite. That's not how the game was played and it was no way to do business in a market where just about everything was questionable. Instead, Papa haggled over the price with the vendor until he got the bracelet for less than it was worth.

No visit to the city was complete without lunching at Qian Men Duck, Peking's most famous restaurant. Their specialty was the delectable Peking Duck. Much to our delight, our Peking hosts offered to take us to this venerable, fourth-generation restaurant. Reservations were made a few days ahead of time so we could feast on this world-famous delicacy. The illustrious duck, which was especially raised, had to be ordered a day in advance. It was a meal not to be taken lightly and required some hours of slow and appreciative consumption.

Everyone in the restaurant loved their Peking Duck, including our happy party. Before the duck was even served, we feasted on the incredibly delicious skin, which had been prepared with spices and roasted to perfection. We ate the skin in special buns before getting to the actual meat and the rest of the trappings. When we entered the restaurant, I noticed that everything was in the open; there was no mysterious kitchen hidden away from the dining room. A large glass panel separated the kitchen area from the ground-floor dining area. Watching the skilled chefs prepare meals was part of the dining experience at Qian Men. Everything seemed to happen in fast forward as chefs dashed around to various work stations. Knives and cleavers flashed through the air, ladles were stirred, soups and sauces were taste-tested, and dashes of pepper and other condiments were added. One got hungry just watching the organized chaos behind the glass wall. Both the main floor and second floor were packed with people enjoying lavish meals. There was a constant flow of customers. As soon as one table of well-fed patrons departed, restaurant staff appeared as if on cue and cleared, cleaned, and reset the table in a matter of minutes. This was the only time a table at Qian Men was vacant.

In addition to showing me all the must-see wonders of Peking, Papa took me to locales that were off the beaten path and rarely frequented by outside visitors. One of these, accessible only by hiring local guides and their donkeys, was an ancient temple located in the hills some miles outside Peking. We left the city on a clear warm day and drove with our friends on unpaved roads to a village at the foot of a steep wooded hill. After some negotiating and bargaining with the owner of these intrepid little beasts of burden, we began an uncomfortable and harrowing journey up the treacherously steep and narrow paths leading to our destination. After some time on the swaying backs of the donkeys, making the dangerous climb up the almost vertical stony inclines, we at last found ourselves at the temple which was surrounded by an ancient, crumbling wall. An equally ancient wooden gate, worn and broken from countless years of service, beckoned us to come inside.

We entered this sacred place and walked in complete silence across a sun-dappled flagstone courtyard. The only sounds to be heard in this haven of tranquillity were those of songbirds chirping happily among the rustling leaves stirring in the light breeze. Decaying steps took us to the massive temple door. Inside we were met by the dusky coolness of bare stone floors; the faint residual odour of incense still perfumed the dry dusty air. We took a few more steps into the confines of the building and were engulfed by complete darkness. By the illuminating beams of our three or four flashlights, the painted temple walls sprang to life. An ancient tableau in vivid colours, preserved in the cool darkness and miraculously undamaged by vandals or curiosity seekers, delighted the eyes and the senses. Scenes of the life of Lord Buddha, rich landscapes, worshipful monks, and strange beasts leapt from the walls. For a short while I was completely captivated by the fervour of these long dead and unknown artists, who so painstakingly decorated the temple. We all stood riveted in silence, each to our own thoughts as the utter magic and beauty of these walls beguiled us. The impatient pawing and whinnying of the donkeys shook us from our transcendental encounter. We retraced our steps to the bright sunlit world outside. Few words were spoken as we began the long journey back to Peking.

As our visit to Peking drew to a close, the disturbing news that the People's Liberation Armies of Mao Tse Tung were swiftly approaching reached us. On the day of our departure we bid our hosts goodbye and left for the airport. We were not alone: it seemed as if half the city, or at least the entire foreign delegation, wanted to flee. The panic-stricken exodus by those who could afford to leave and were able to obtain tickets created chaos at the airport. Plane after plane taxied from the terminal and lined up at the runway, taking off as soon as the plane ahead was airborne. This pace had been going on for days, underscoring the magnitude of the mass departure. When our flight finally left, it was one of the last flights to become airborne before the airport was surrounded by Communist troops and finally closed. Once in the air, our return trip was much less eventful than the flight to Peking. Despite the wonders I had seen in the nation's capital, I was glad to arrive back in Shanghai.

Opa's imminent death made our homecoming sad and full of foreboding. It was October 12, 1948, when we touched down at the airport in Shanghai. Mama anxiously awaited our return, as she worried about our safety the entire time we were gone. She met us at the airport. At once I noticed how tired and drained she looked. Lack of sleep from keeping vigil at Opa's bedside had painted dark circles around her eyes. Seeing Papa and me emerge from the arrival gate, however, drew a happy, relieved smile from her. We all hugged. I had not felt this close to Mama and Papa in a long time. The first thing I asked her was about Opa's health. "I'm afraid he is not well, my darling, and won't be with us much longer," she said, not trying to hide the fact she was about to lose her father and my beloved Opa. "He has been asking about you. We'll go and see him later today."

I wanted to go to the hospital right from the airport, but Mama suggested Papa and I should go home first to freshen up and drop off our luggage. On what turned out to be my last visit to Opa's bedside, he managed to smile and gently touch my face in a final gesture of love. I could not bear to leave the hospital, but we were told that visiting hours were over and that we had to go. I knew in my heart that I had just said my final farewell to the dear man who had been the cornerstone of my life in Shanghai. A few hours later Mama and Papa were summoned back to the hospital; the light of my life for so many years was gone. I had seen much death during my short years on earth but Opa's passing devastated me. I felt a permanent sense of loss for this kind and gentle man who had provided me with so many years of companionship and love.

Now that Opa was gone, I believed that I should have inherited his bedroom; however, this was not to be the case. It had been decided that Papa's helper Foo Dor and his wife would move in with us. They were assigned Opa's room. I was deeply hurt since I had no say in the matter and resigned myself to remaining in the master bedroom's cramped alcove.

Stephen and Foo Dor's son, April 16, 1950

I reluctantly returned to my classes at the Shanghai Jewish School and had to work hard to catch up on missed lessons. I was bored stiff with the rigidity of the formal education system and daydreamed about the excitement of the recent trip to Peking. Why could not all learning be as fun as field trips and the reality of life on the streets? A new unexpected sparkle, however, was about to change my perception of the tediousness of being an average 12-year-old schoolgirl who was forced to endure agonizing hours of classroom captivity.

A young Chinese officer who was attached to the airport security forces in Shanghai had noticed me as Papa and I left for Peking. A few weeks after our return, the officer found Papa and asked if he might be permitted to come on Saturdays to escort me out. I can not imagine what that conversation might have entailed or what was promised, but my Saturdays were now to be spent in the company of this friendly and totally undemanding person named Hsia. I was unable to satisfy my curiosity over this strange arrangement. Why Hsia wanted my particular company would always remain a mystery to me, but he assured Papa that his intentions were honourable. True to his word, he was in every sense of the definition an officer and a gentleman; he very carefully avoided making any advances toward me. Hsia was perfectly content in taking me to fine restaurants, to movies, for walks along the Bund, and on outings to the countryside in his fancy car. I really did enjoy my Saturdays with him and felt flattered by his many expensive gifts. He spoke no English and he was happy that I was able to speak the local dialect, although at times my accent and limited command of the language amused him. I was not offended when he laughed at something silly I may have said. Rather, his laughter was contagious and I laughed with him.

My attempts at questioning Mama and Papa about Hsia were met by a change in subject or plain silence, so I eventually gave up. I later ascertained that because Hsia was a high-ranking officer he was able to smooth over some bureaucratic entanglements Papa was facing. During this time Papa, seeing the writing on the wall and partly at the urging of Hsia, began sending his most valuable books, including some rare Chinese manuscripts, out of the country to Kurt Schwartz in San Francisco for safekeeping.

The beginning of 1949 saw the escalation of political uncertainty and the continued successes of the People's Liberation Army in their movement to the south. By the end of January, Peking had totally fallen under control of the Communists. Although fierce fighting had raged in and around Peking since Papa and I had made our hasty exit, saner heads prevailed in the end. General Fu Zuoyi, the Nationalist commander in charge of guarding the ancient city, accepted a Communist proposal for peaceful liberation, saving it from catastrophic damages. An unsettling story began circulating around Shanghai that, for many, meant the beginning of the end was surely near. A huge cache of arms that had been left behind in the city of Tientsin by retreating Nationalist troops gave the Communists an unexpected boost in their fight to become the new masters of China. The feelings of uncertainty that covered Shanghai like a dark, heavy blanket prevailed and put everyone on edge. Promises by the mayor of Shanghai to defend China's largest city to the last drop of blood did very little to calm the jitters of the business community and the general population. Foreign interests prepared to pull out of the city and the Nationalist government found it increasingly more difficult to prop up its shaky currency.

For me, life remained a cycle of school, sneaking into the Uptown Theatre, and Saturdays with Hsia. I seemed to have my own little world perfectly under control. But on a blustery and rainy day in January, Papa quite unexpectedly came to fetch me at the end of the school day. From his unusually stone cold expression, I knew that something was definitely amiss. I was racking my brain trying to figure out which of my unauthorized exploits had come to light. Any attempt at conversation was stifled by monosyllables. Upon our arrival home, Papa faced me angrily and demanded an explanation for my absence at school some days before. I assumed he was putting on this front for Mama who, with crossed arms in front of her, fixed me with a harsh gaze and waited for a reply. I was relieved it was only my playing hooky that had reached their ears, but I was annoyed that some busybody, who apparently had spotted me on the street during school hours with a friend, reported this to Mama and Papa. I admitted my truancy that day with what I thought was a perfectly reasonable explanation: it was a boring assembly day, and seeing that I was not going to miss much actual school work I decided not to attend.

More anger erupted. Considering the cost of keeping me in school, it was quite reasonably so. "I'm glad Opa is no longer with us so he isn't here to witness this travesty," Mama said as if I had just committed the worst of crimes. She really knew how to push my guilt button with the mention of Opa. So with the most earnest of promises, and sincerest of apologies that I could possibly dredge from the reserve I kept in my mind for exactly these kinds of situations, the storm eventually abated. "Well, that's just fine Hannah, and you certainly are getting better at showing remorse, I must say. Although I still question just how valid it is. Now go to your room," Papa said and pointed in the direction of the master bedroom, as if I needed a reminder of which direction to follow. "What about supper? I'm hungry," I quipped over my shoulder. "Lots of poor unfortunate children go to bed hungry every night. Tonight you will be one of them," retorted Papa.

"So much for that tune," I thought. But no problem, as I had a little stash of chestnuts and a few other goodies hidden away for just these situations. It was not the first time I had been punished with the old "no supper routine."

My meetings with Hsia continued, though not as often, and he seemed more and more preoccupied. I asked him how the Communist takeover would affect his life, but he said that those were not things with which I should concern myself. I told him I was concerned and I knew he was touched; although, like any well-trained officer, he did his best not to let his emotions show. In early March, he announced he had been ordered to vacate Shanghai within a few days. The dreary weather was a perfect complement for this terrible news. I was sorry to hear he had to leave and that this strange interlude in my life would draw to a close.

On the surface there appeared to be little change in our daily lives. It was almost like the calm before the storm. Life in the city continued in its usual noisy, bustling way. Mama and Papa still spent many of their evenings either entertaining or being entertained by friends, though the numbers were fast dwindling. The biggest rush to leave Shanghai since the end of the war was now in progress. In what turned out to be the last few weeks of Shanghai under Nationalist control, the economic situation grew more chaotic by the day. The population of the city faced full-scale inflation, with panic-stricken people carrying more and more satchels and bags of useless paper money each time they went shopping. Some employers were paying their employees two or three times a day so they could still purchase the necessities of life before the prices escalated again. At banks, the daily crushing line-ups of people desperately trying to exchange their worthless currency was caught in the now famous photo by the French photographer Henri Cartier Bresson.

For Mama and Papa, the all pervading aura that hung over Shanghai was reminiscent of the dire times of post-World War II Berlin. Instead of a fascist Nazi regime lurking in the wings, it was the spectre of an almost equally dreaded Communist horde which threatened to spin our lives in a new and uncertain direction. Papa tried to maintain his business and livelihood even though many of his customers had joined in the exodus. Still, in keeping with his persona, he maintained a cheerful, optimistic outlook for the future: he had no plans to leave the country, as yet. Though the opportunity to return to Germany and regain German citizenships was there for Mama and Papa to consider, they steadfastly rejected that option. Under no circumstance did they wish to return to a country with such a bloody wartime record.

In the outlying countryside, meanwhile, the hardships and hunger continued to increase. Peasants were reduced to cooking grasses and bark off the trees or flocking to nearby towns and cities to pick through the garbage on the streets. In the face of this ever-worsening situation, the desperate villagers were welcoming the People's Liberation Army as saviours sent by their honourable ancestors. The villagers, with their primitive weapons, simple cotton uniforms, and straw sandals, were more than happy to join the victorious troops. Shanghai, a city that had seen its share of upheaval in the past few decades, prepared for battle.

On the outskirts of the city, storage facilities for gasoline and oil tanks were set on fire, lighting up the night sky in an eerie panorama of crimson and orange. The sounds of mortar fire and heavy armaments sounded in the distance. Sandbags appeared on street corners, and merchants prepared to paper or board up their store windows. The city held its breath while people, though nervous and apprehensive, tried to live their lives as normally as possible in a world that was anything but normal. I still made my way to school daily, though everyone was abuzz over the impending events.

May 1, 1949, dawned clear and warm, and remarkably silent. There were no gunshots, no mortars fired; none of the sounds of terror that accompany an invasion were heard. The promised battle for Shanghai did not materialize. The armies of Chang Kai Shek, knowing the futility of resistance, perhaps, had quietly melted into the population of the city or moved further south where the Nationalists still held some sway. Down Nanking Road, Shanghai's main thoroughfare, the new occupation army, this time not foreign like the Japanese before them, marched with quiet deliberation and an obvious sense of victory. It was with relief that people realized there had been no loss of civilian life. This takeover by the Communists was accomplished without the usual episodes of looting, rape, and disorderly conduct that are the earmark of a victorious army. For the first few weeks, the citizens breathed a collective sigh of relief and continued to live their lives.

Shanghai and its inhabitants awaited the momentous changes that would come about with the establishment of a new regime by the Communists. Some of Shanghai's citizens waited the changes with eager anticipation, some with dread, and others with jaded indifference.

LIFE UNDER THE COMMUNISTS

By the middle of May 1949, Shanghai and the surrounding countryside were firmly under Communist control, and some five million people were waiting for the other shoe to drop. When the People's Liberation Army first entered the city, the effect was one of anxiety and a comedy of errors. Many of its soldiers, who either volunteered or were recruited from country villages, had never been to a large western-style city like Shanghai. They were truly out of their element and confounded by much of what they encountered. One of the objects that perplexed many of the rag-tag soldiers was the modern flush toilet. They had no idea what purpose this strange contraption served. One of its possible uses, they deduced, was to wash rice before cooking. Accordingly, rice was poured into the bowl, the chain pulled, with the rice disappearing in the process; no amount of waiting brought it back. Eventually they were informed of the toilet's real use.

The traffic chaos on the busy city streets was intimidating for many members of the victorious army. Some of these soldiers had never seen trucks or cars until the Communists pulled into their villages. For them, a busy road meant a number of oxen-pulled carts approaching a village intersection at the same time. They were afraid to cross the streets of the modern city. They marvelled at the effect that the changing coloured traffic lights had on the movement of the vehicles. They were dumbfounded by the height of buildings such as the Hong Kong-Shanghai Bank, with its spectacular dome-shaped roof; the Custom House situated along the Bund, with its famous skyward-reaching clock tower; and the ultra-modern Grosvenor Apartments complex. Some soldiers feared of being crushed by what they believed was the imminent collapse of these structures and avoided walking near them. The antics of these peasant soldiers added some comic relief to the drama that had Shanghai in its grip, but the seriousness of the situation hardly abated. The changes that were already rampant in other areas of China began to filter slowly into the city's consciousness, setting an ominous agenda for decades to come.

At the outset the changes were, for the most part, of a positive nature, especially for the poorest of the poor. For the elite classes, however, the changes would prove most cataclysmic. The problems facing the new regime, which had proclaimed itself the People's Republic of China in October 1949, were overwhelming and diverse. The near-starving population of beggars, destitute farmers, and bankrupt small business owners became a challenge to the new regime. Mounds of rotting garbage clogged the streets. The ever-present danger of rampant epidemic diseases and of medical facilities unable to handle the large numbers of ailing and needy, in addition to the logistics of keeping a city like Shanghai running, were just some of the pressing issues that required urgent attention. The new government moved with surprising speed to stabilize the worthless currency and save what was left of the comatose economy of Shanghai. Metre by metre, and block by block, the streets were cleared of the mountains of filthy rotting garbage. Next, the massive number of beggars were relocated. Every doctor practising in the city had to devote a number of hours each day dealing with the poor and homeless sick.

Although these, and other obvious changes, were clearly an improvement in people's lives, Shanghai's citizens were soon to experience the other side of the coin. Any foreign-owned and operated businesses that had not already left the city were now in the process of departing. Shanghai, once the third busiest and largest commercial harbour in Asia, was fast dwindling to a few British freighters and some other international shipping. Britain had been one of the first nations to recognize China's new regime. This enabled Britain to continue its long and prosperous trade relationship with China.

While the rest of the country was slowly withdrawing from western culture and other influences, Shanghai, too, was beginning to feel the transformation as new laws and edicts made it even more uncomfortable for foreigners to remain. The new regime made its anti-western sentiments felt in no uncertain terms. Western-style fashions were discouraged in favour of the plain cotton pants, shirts, and jackets similar to the ones worn by members of the army. School children were ordered to wear uniforms consisting of white shirts, dark coloured pants or skirts, and the soon-to-become trademark red scarf or large bandana knotted around the neck. The once colourful streets had become lacklustre as more and more stores ceased to display imported or locally manufactured luxury goods. It was as if banality had become high fashion; China was regressing into a homogenous, drab society.

Individuality and freethinking were discouraged, too. Soon it would not be tolerated at all. Although an official curfew was never imposed upon the populace, the closure of nearly all places of entertainment such as nightclubs, theatres, cinemas, ballrooms, and popular restaurants kept most people at home, including Mama and Papa. As had been my nature since I had been old enough to understand the vagaries of human existence, I tried to ignore all that did not directly affect me and continued to live life as an adventure. There were too many things to do, and too many things to see and experience. Besides, I had never known anything but extremes and upheaval; the Communists just brought a different slant to things.

More and more, the streets were filled with roaming vehicles equipped with loudspeakers that blared slogans and messages glorifying the revolution and the newfound happiness of the people under Communism. Billboards covered by political cartoons and anti-Western sentiments were found on many street corners. The large American paint company across the street from our home was turned into a roller-skating rink. This change was representative of the times–if it was western it had to go! Patriotic music blasted in both Chinese and Russian from loudspeakers located on the outside of the new roller rink. This continual bombardment of enervating sound became difficult to live with, particularly for those unaccustomed to Far Eastern music.

Within a very short period of time, thousands of enthusiastic people, primarily the very young and school-aged children, were out on the streets parading with huge banners, flags, and portraits of Chairman Mao and other leaders of the government. These long and noisy parades were usually headed by persons with loud voices and bull-horns, leading the followers with songs, exhortations, and threats to the enemies of the people. For Mama and Papa, and any of the former refugees still in the city, the scenes unfolding in Shanghai stirred memories of a similar kind of blind fanaticism: that which had spawned Nazi Germany. But now it was not an issue of being Jewish, but it was simply of not being Chinese: Communist Chinese!

It seemed that once again, the inmates had taken over the asylum. This time it was in a different place, a different time, and with different people playing the roles. The lowest common denominator, however, remained the same: madness and oppression. The daily migration of a significant number of people winding through the streets brought traffic to a standstill and kept many foreigners indoors. Fear and panic became the order of the day for many; it was a distressing way of life that had dire consequences. Those events, in addition to new government-imposed restrictions affecting Papa's business and the departure of friends and loyal customers, virtually brought the Western Arts Gallery to an end. At this time, however, he still had permission to import scholarly books into the country to supply Chinese universities with up-to-date scientific and medical materials. Papa still kept food on our table.

In spite of these difficulties and marginal income, Mama, whose health always hung in a precarious balance, was able to retain the services of a loyal and helpful Amah. Although she was only thirty-five years old, Amah, meaning "nanny" in Mandarin and the only name by which I ever knew her, already had brought fifteen children of her own into the world in as many years. She was married to an abusive and demanding man. She desperately needed the pittance Papa was able to pay her so she could help keep her family alive. Amah not only cooked and cleaned, but she also took three-year-old Stephen under her wing. As she spoke no English, he very quickly picked up the local Chinese dialect from her, and he and I often spoke to each other in the language neither of my parents could understand. Amah was like a second mother to Stephen. Sometimes, she took him home to play with her own children and partake in a meagre meal. As my experiences as a child in wartime Shanghai had been deemed an adventure, so were these times to my little brother.

Meanwhile, I had transferred to yet another school. With not enough Jewish children left in the city, the Shanghai Jewish School had closed its doors. The British educators who ran my new school taught the necessary courses so their pupils could sit for the final matriculation exams set by Cambridge University in England. I would attend this school for only one year before it, too, was closed.

The few foreigners who were still in business were now facing daily increases in restrictions and anti-foreign sentiments. As these grew ever more strident, Mama and Papa were finally convinced that we could no longer hope to survive in this uncomfortable political climate. With the bookshop's closure now imminent, and the prospects of making any other kind of living next to zero, we seriously had to consider leaving the country. We had relatives, the Beckers and Gadiels, who lived in Canada and were more than willing to sponsor us; thus, the possibility of emigrating to this new land was open to us. Both families were among our more fortunate relatives to have escaped the Holocaust. They had made their way to the prairie province of Manitoba via Buenos Aires in Argentina, where they spent the war years. The Beckers and Gadiels were cousins to Mama and part of Opa's extended family. They had been urging us to join them in their new homeland which they said was about as close to the land of milk and honey as could be. Papa, however, also considered an invitation from his sister, Ellen, who lived in New York. She had lived there since 1936 and had assured him that his book business would thrive in the cosmopolitan city. As it turned out, to emigrate to the United States involved much more red tape than the country north of its border. Canada became the obvious choice. Accordingly, we began the long process of applying for entry into a country of which we knew very little. For Mama and Papa, this was the end of their dream to spend the rest of their lives in China. It was truly a bitter pill to swallow. They had come to love this country and felt as one with its people. Because I had only fragmented memories of Berlin and Germany, for me the prospect of leaving Shanghai was, in a way, even more devastating. It was the only city I had ever truly known. Even though I had not been born here, I was very much a product of Shanghai. I considered myself a Shanghailander.

All available plots of land were used to grow vegetables to feed the Liberation Army. My own little Garden of Eden, the wild and beautiful Hardoun property, was no exception. When after a year or so I was able to get back onto the property, I found myself looking in disbelief at a vista of complete desolation and could not help but break into tears. The lovely lake, every tree, the profusion of wild plants, and each blade of grass had totally disappeared. All previous vegetation had been replaced by dry brown earth and a few rows of wilting vegetables. The transformation was completely and utterly sad, like the transformation that was taking place in our lives.

The rapid changes overtaking us had real and dire consequences for many people. As the state slowly usurped the place of the family, and the system proclaimed itself the most important part of one's daily existence, individual freedoms came to an end. School children were trained to inform on their parents, and the slightest infraction of the new laws was followed by arrests and harassment. Neighbours or anyone with an axe to grind who informed on their victims were rewarded for their betrayal. Children openly declared their loyalty to the state and scolded their parents for not displaying more enthusiasm or embracing the new ideals that were taking root.

The millennia-old social fabric of the country was unravelling; family values were disintegrating like sandcastles caught in a rising tide. Many older people, who were unable to adjust to the "new society" took desperate means to escape. Before Communism enveloped China, one was hardly aware of anti-social behaviour due to psychological stress. Though many encountered problems living under difficult situations, there had always been the security of family and community to fall back on. This safety net had started to collapse and quickly disappeared along with the rest of old China. The desperation of those who felt themselves to be in danger of arrest, sometimes for something as trivial as listening to short-wave radio or hoarding food or money, resulted in many people seeking to escape by committing suicide. Incidents of suicide among the Chinese had been virtually unheard of, but they had started to become a frightening reality. Entire families shared a meal in which every dish had been poisoned, individuals jumped to their deaths from high-rise buildings, or others desperately throwing themselves in front of trains became an almost daily occurrence.

We also began to notice more and more cultural and artistic activity coming to an end. As the government became completely committed to a new industrial revolution, many buildings that had once housed places of entertainment were converted into factories. Some artists, writers, and teachers were obliged to undergo retraining as factory workers; others were sent into the fields to help the farmers. We were witnessing the early stages of what would become China's Cultural Revolution which would later bring so much suffering and have such a tremendously adverse effect upon the country's educational, cultural, and scientific advancements. At the height of this craziness, thousands of young people no longer interested in school or university educations criss-crossed the country proclaiming their anti-cultural feelings. Quite often they physically attacked anyone who advocated a less radical approach. Even people wearing eyeglasses were thought to be intellectuals and were subjected to beatings and other abusive behaviours. I had heard about the horrors of Nazi Germany, endured the Japanese occupation of Shanghai, and survived the deprivations of the Hongkew ghetto, believing that the end of World War II was the end of madness. I realized then that madness had no time limit, knew no bounds, and thrived by feeding upon itself.

In the neighbourhood where I lived, cadres of young students were organized to go from house to house and inspect the premises for cleanliness and the absence of vermin. Every household became responsible for the capture and extermination of rats, cockroaches, and even flies. Rewards of money were offered for the eradication of these pests. This edict almost turned this old, filthy but character-rich city into a clean and sanitized place. Shanghai's very heart and soul had come close to being covered over with a thin veneer of disinfectant. While life in the city was arduous at best, in villages and farms across the country a macabre theatre of vengeance took place. Landowners were arrested and without much formality or regard for due process were marched in chains to public squares where they faced kangaroo courts. These were presided over by former tenants and, often, badly treated farm labourers. If the landowner had been particularly abusive toward the farmers on his land, justice was summary and the offender was shot right there and then. Those considered to be enlightened souls were given amnesty, but they were stripped of all their properties and re-educated to work alongside former serfs. Black market vendors were especially sought out with no mercy in store for them. When discovered, quite often by the betrayal of a former customer, they were executed on the spot. In the larger cities, people were obliged by edict to resettle remote areas of the country in order to develop, cultivate, and establish new communities. Some two million people, mostly young, were sent from Shanghai to these remote areas. They often had to leave behind elderly parents, burdened wives, and young children. For the old, this edict was tantamount to a death sentence, as they had no one to look after their needs once their children were gone.

Mama and Papa, who were now fully committed to leaving this increasingly hostile country, were kept busy fulfilling the requirements to obtain Canadian visas. They had to fill out interminable forms, pass strict medical exams, and make numerous visits to the British Consulate, which was in charge of Canadian affairs in Shanghai. When we finally received permission to emigrate to the Dominion of Canada, there was a sense of relief mixed with sadness among us. Once again, we were being uprooted. Once again, we did not know what was in store for us. We had been assured that the country that lay north of the American border was a land of the future, a land of immigrants.

Much time was spent deciding what to pack for a country we practically knew nothing about. What would the Chinese authorities permit us to take out of the country? It was like Berlin all over again except this time the oppressors were Communists instead of Nazis. It did not matter, however, as the experience of the oppressed remained one of humiliation, hopelessness, and the stripping of dignity. Every personal item had to be described in detail. All papers, photos, memorabilia, books, and items of clothing were listed and examined. Then, under close observation, everything was packed into crates to be shipped to Canada. This process took weeks. Finally, the only things left were to be stuffed into three or four suitcases. Many of our belongings were confiscated and did not receive the official seal or tag assigned to possessions permitted to leave the country. Although Opa was not around to entertain and distract the inspectors this time, Mama still managed to conceal a number of valuable collectibles and pieces of artwork, including paintings by her friend Lin Fu Ming, one of the renowned artists of the city. Mama and Papa were once again faced with having to leave behind a home complete with all its furnishings and household goods. Papa had to leave a store filled with books. Their favourite table, which had seen countless moves from Berlin on, would have to stay behind. We were about to close the door behind us and walk away to an uncertain life. Canada beckoned us with the distant light of new opportunities and the wonderful promise of freedom. I was about to embark on a new adventure. Or, so I believed.

THE SPY

The bittersweet excitement of our imminent departure was taking hold. Our plans were finalized. Our departure date was set for December 5, 1951. All that remained was the decision of what to pack in our four suitcases.

Mama, Hannelore, Stephen, and Papa, 1951

I thought a lot about Canada, the land where I would probably spend the rest of my life. As a 15-year-old girl, what would I do there? Would I fall in love with a handsome young Canadian, or would I meet an immigrant like myself? Would he be Jewish, Christian, or of another faith? Did I really care? Love and romance was what seemed to be occupying my mind a lot these days. I wondered, too, if Papa would finally be able to nurture a lasting book business: one that he would enjoy and reap the benefits of for the rest of his life, especially after what happened in Berlin and in Shanghai. Would Mama's health improve? Surely the weather in Canada would be more agreeable to her. I thought a lot about Opa, too. I wished he was still alive and going with us to our new haven of safety. The thought of leaving him behind in his final resting place in Shanghai disheartened me. I came to realize exactly how Opa must have felt about leaving behind the grave of his beloved wife.

As we waited for our date of departure, Papa closed his business. He had kept it open despite the fact that many of his regular customers had left. There were almost no westerners left in Shanghai, and the cultured and well-read Chinese who frequented the bookstore in the past had disappeared. They feared the displeasure of the authorities who frowned on any Chinese still doing business with westerners. The store was boarded up, its façade looking like an abandoned dwelling that belonged in a ghost town. Although we still lived upstairs, the life and spirit had been drained from the place. There was nothing more to hold us there.

Our exit visas stated that we were to leave by train for Canton, a most uncomfortable journey of three days. Once the police had cleared us in Canton, we were to cross by foot into the no man's land that separated China from the British Colony of Hong Kong. We would only be truly free once we stepped on to British soil. Not only would we be sitting upright for the entire trip, but the supply of meals would be uncertain. To add to our unease and anxiety, we heard horror stories circulating of foreigners being harassed en route and, upon arrival in Canton, being subjected to ill treatment by the police. There were even stories about authorities shooting departing travellers as they left China. None of this, however, dampened our optimism, especially Papa, who remained the most optimistic of men. Besides, Mama and Papa had seen their paradise turn into hell before and had moved on to survive in another part of the world: they were old hands at it now. Although they wished Shanghai could have become their permanent home, they were prepared to start all over once more. I truly admired their resilience and their strength to deal with situations that had proved to be the finality of many a weaker person. Their optimism and positive outlook on life was not lost on me, and I was happy enough to bid the few friends I was leaving a fond farewell. I knew the time had come to start another chapter in my life.

The departure date approached and we were mentally and physically ready to undertake the long journey that would take us to Canada. On December 3, we were totally stunned when informed that our exit visas had been cancelled. This news had the effect of a verbal hand grenade exploding in the mind. No explanation was given and a sense of foreboding swept over us like fog rolling in off the harbour. We were not to be held in suspense for long. On the morning of December 5, Mama left home early to make the trip to the British Consulate to inform the officials of the unanticipated delay to our plans. Papa remained with me and was preoccupied with his thoughts.

While out of view, in the bathroom, I was suddenly startled by loud footsteps and angry voices. Upon entering the living room, I found to my horror and surprise a small group of men in uniform who were armed to the teeth. They were informing Papa that he was being arrested and to ready himself for departure. "Do not try and escape. You will be shot at once," yelled one of the men for good measure, in very poor English. I could not believe what was happening: my jaw dropped. I wanted to scream at these men to get out and leave my dear father alone. But the words did not come. It was as if my vocal chords had been anaesthetized. Papa sensed my despair and was highly agitated, a state I had rarely seen him in. He was no doubt worried that his outspoken daughter would complicate matters; his taut facial expression and body language suggested he was anxious that I should leave the room. I hesitated a moment because I did not want to leave him, but his pleading looks made me decide to wait for him downstairs at the front door, from which he and the Communist soldiers would have to depart. A short time later he emerged from upstairs surrounded by his guards. "Tell your mother not to worry." Those were Papa's last words. The guards ordered him to be silent and hustled him to a curtained vehicle waiting outside. They aggressively pushed Papa inside the car and whisked him away.

Amah, who had been busy with the care of Stephen, was visibly shocked by what had transpired. The uniformed men had barked some questions at her and then dismissed her. She retreated in silence to the kitchen, shaking her head and looking rather fearful. Some time later, Mama returned and immediately sensed something was amiss.

"What's going on here? Why does everybody look so glum? Where's Papa? Has something happened to him?" she asked me, noticing I had started to choke back tears. In between sobs I told her of the events of the morning. To my surprise she appeared to take it calmly enough, but as time passed she began to realize the enormity of Papa's arrest. She became more and more disconcerted, and I was afraid she was going to unravel completely. I decided to phone one of her friends to tell her that Mama was not well and asked if she could please come over.

As we all sat and discussed the situation, not knowing what the next action should be, two policemen arrived and "requested" that Mama sign a paper stating she was aware her husband had been arrested. "You'd better pack some blankets, warm clothing, and soap and deliver them to the police station. Your husband will need them. They are not provided by the state," one of the officers told her. His English was much better than that of the earlier intruders. No further information was supplied; Mama's anxious questions regarding the reasons for Papa's arrest were ignored. She burst into tears after the police left. Uncertainty was now taking over: two young children, no visible means of income, a husband who was under arrest in a dictatorial country, and, worst of all, we were still stateless entities with no consulate to come to our rescue. It was a frightening situation. Unlike the drama in Berlin, from which my tender years protected me, I was now old enough to understand that what was happening was not a good thing, to say the least. Mama's behaviour became idiosyncratic, and one of the first repercussions of Papa's arrest was that she refused to sleep in their bed. Instead, she spent a sleepless night on the living room couch, weeping and wailing till dawn. I was powerless to help. I, too, spent the night tossing and turning, wondering what would happen next.

The following day brought an old friend to our door to assist us. It was Dr. Hans Blaschauer, a crusty old bachelor and Jewish scholar who was fluent in Greek and Latin, and was a lawyer by profession. Dr. Blaschauer, "B" for short, was an Old China hand who had lived in Shanghai for many years, having belonged to the first wave of escapees from Nazi Germany. Like most people we had come to know in the city, he had ventured into our lives through Papa's bookshop. Despite his esteemed professional status, B was a simple man whose needs and wants were few. He occupied a little corner in a house owned by Chinese friends and mostly shunned the trappings of the material world. Like my gypsy friends from bygone days, B lived very much in the moment.

Dr. Hans Blaschauer and student, April 1950

Because the mass post-war migration of westerners had left his law practice with few clients, B had taken up teaching Latin, Greek, and English to Chinese students. "I would like to suggest that seeing as the bookshop is closed, I could use the space as a classroom," he told Mama over a cup of coffee. "You would be helping me out and I, in turn, can help you out a little." It was fairly obvious that his proposal was a guise for Mama to save face. Any money was welcomed, however, and an arrangement was instantly made for him to use the premises. Although he earned only a pittance from his teaching job, he was more than willing to share most of his earnings with us. Without a doubt, B was our saviour and he proved to be a pillar of support for Mama. His sense of humour and unfailing optimism cheered and encouraged her, yet she continued to spend her nights on the couch and in tears. For the next six months we lived in a state of uncertainty and sheer terror.

Unbeknownst to us at that time, Papa was being held in total isolation with his hands and feet manacled to a wall. Eventually this bondage caused him to suffer very painful circulation problems. Meals for him consisted of rice gruel with occasional second-rate vegetables and never any meat or fruit. Miraculously he was not subjected to physical torture, but the isolation proved to be the worst experience of his life. Papa was the most sociable of people, used to interacting with persons of all walks of life in his bookshop. To be deprived of human contact was unbearable for him. Sometimes he was allowed to leave his cell but only to be questioned for hours on end by his captors. Despite his enthusiastic and positive personality, which without question helped him survive, he fell into a deep depression. He clung to sanity by doing mental exercises like imaginary games of chess, composing music in his head, creating a novel based on his life, and recalling every book he had ever sold and to whom.

After six months of solitary confinement, Papa was finally moved from his small, dungeon-like cell to a larger enclosure that housed eleven other prisoners, including a Tibetan nobleman. Because Papa spoke no Chinese, he was unable to communicate verbally with his fellow inmates. However, just being around other people was like an elixir for him. Sign and body language overcame the language barrier and, in time, he picked up a few Chinese words and phrases. Papa was now able to move around, albeit in a confined space. He and his roommates, as he preferred to call them, got along well and they took pride in keeping their cell absolutely clean. "You could have eaten off the floor," Papa later told us. He was also fed a better diet, which, nonetheless, he was barely able to subsist on. This food, and the horrible slop which had been fed to him in isolation, eventually led to a severe case of beriberi.

Throughout this period of uncertainty, we still did not know why Papa was being detained and, worse, whether he was even alive. Mama repeatedly asked the authorities for information about him until, one day, finally they informed her that she would be allowed to deliver some necessities for him every month. Although they did not mention a thing about his well being, if he had been charged, or if he had been brought to trial, we at least knew he was still alive. This was the most welcomed news we could have received. We both felt like an immense weight had been lifted off our shoulders, and it restored some hope in us that eventually everything would work out. And so we entered a new phase in our confrontation with the Communist regime.

Mama made a list of what she brought to the prison each time she went to visit Papa: a change of clothes, a bar of soap, a piece of fruit, etc. He was not allowed cigarettes, books, or writing materials. These were considered unnecessary comforts and comfort was not on the agenda. Mama cleverly insisted that she wanted to receive Papa's signature on the list of goods she brought so she knew he had received them. Although there was no guarantee that he did indeed receive the items, she knew by his signature that he was actually alive and being held nearby. Mama had studied graphology years earlier and was quite adept at interpreting handwriting. She could also ascertain some inkling of his well being from the form of his signature. Fortunately, the authorities agreed to her request. After waiting for approximately half an hour in a designated room, which was in keeping with the general gloom of the prison, the list was returned to her with Papa's signature. This paper was all the evidence she needed to know that, at least for the present, the strength of his signature conveyed he was all right. During the full term of his confinement, however, his signature would fluctuate from almost normal to an almost unintelligible scribble.

Through the westerner's grapevine, a veritable lifeline for those of us who had remained behind in Shanghai, Mama heard of a German butcher who was still operating a sausage manufacturing plant. She learned that he needed someone to sell and deliver his wares among the few remaining Europeans still in the city. I willingly offered to do this job because we were in dire need of money and I wanted to contribute whatever I could. With Mama's somewhat reluctant blessing I went and applied for the job. Mama knew the money I would be able to earn would greatly help, but at the same time she had reservations about me traipsing all over Shanghai delivering sausages. Apparently nobody else had shown any interest in the job and I was promptly hired. Once again life took on a new aspect for me; it may have been work, but it was not without its interesting moments. I left home early in the morning, travelled by streetcar to the butcher's location on the outskirts of town, picked up an assortment of tasty European meat delicacies, and set out on my daily rounds. The butcher was able to supply me with the names of current customers, but it soon became apparent that many more were required to make this a viable enterprise because I was paid only on the product I delivered. I, therefore, made it my business to find and approach as many foreigners as possible who might have a taste for this staple of German foods. I was unable to acquire any Chinese customers because they found things like sausages totally disgusting and inedible. A sizable market was thus unobtainable to me and the sausage delivery business was anything but a feasible and profitable venture.

Many of the people I approached knew my family and were aware of the circumstances in which we found ourselves. I was both surprised and dumbstruck by the number of so-called friends and acquaintances who reacted with either embarrassment, fear of knowing me, or both. They glanced nervously over my shoulder into the street, to the left and to the right, as if making sure there were no police or military types lurking about ready to pounce on them because I had come to their home. When they felt confident I was not being shadowed like some common criminal looking for a place to hide, they politely but firmly asked me not to return. "We'd love to help you and your mother, dear, but you must understand that under the circumstances we just can't do anything for you." This was the patronizing line I became accustomed to hearing. I almost came to expect it. When I told these people that I did not understand, I was usually answered with the door being slammed in my face.

I was learning cold hard lessons about the world of adults, about a world into which I was rapidly growing up; but I did not become disillusioned by this unfair treatment. I understood that consorting with the daughter of an imprisoned man might send out the wrong signals to the authorities. Many times I had heard from Mama and Papa, when they told me not to hang out with a certain person: "Show me your friends and I'll show you who you are." Perhaps that worn cliché bore some truth. It was indeed a strange world we inhabited; and right then no place seemed stranger than Shanghai, which even in the best of times had never been a conventional town.

I did make it a point to adopt some of Papa's positive outlook on life, and my faith in humanity was quickly enough restored. Complete strangers were often most welcoming and obliging to help. They did not know my situation and my family's real or imagined wrongdoings against the Communist regime. So, despite the scarcity of a viable customer base, I was able to earn a few pennies here and there, which eased the plight Mama, Stephen, and I faced. The butcher's willingness to throw in an occasional ham or sausage as a bonus was greatly appreciated, too.

Still, the enterprise was so financially unrewarding that I knew something had to be done, and once again I proved to be my father's daughter. To augment our income that cold winter of our discontent, I suggested to Mama that she put her culinary talents to good use so that I could add some non-meat products to my line of butcher's goods. "Why, Hannelore, that is an excellent idea," Mama said with no lack of pride. "I know exactly what to make, inexpensive but delicious and certain to fetch a bit of a profit." We were in business. Mama's goodies proved to be a hit with many of my customers. One of her specialties was *kochkäse*, a mouth-watering cheese spread that went exceptionally well with dark rye bread. She made this spread by boiling unpasteurised cottage cheese. Mama was in possession of a recipe that had been passed down to her by her grandmother. The secret to making an exceptional kochkäse, she told me, was a blend of herbs and spices including caraway seeds. Although relatively simple to make, it was nonetheless a time-consuming process that required loving care and attention. Also included in Mama's wares were German cookies and other baked delicacies. One did not really equate sweets and sausages coming from the same vendor, but my customers were quite receptive to the baked goods.

Dr. Blaschauer, meanwhile, continued to give language lessons in the former Western Arts Gallery. It was now the winter of 1951 and he and his students were bundled up in the chilly rooms of the store, shivering but willing to put up with the discomforts. B emerged from the lessons with the occasional amusing anecdote, which usually got Mama laughing. One day, he told us about giving a student the definition of a bachelor, which he explained by saying that a "bachelor lived like a king but died like a dog." There was a moment's silence, he said, and then the student piped up and asked whether one could say that a spinster lived like a queen, but died like a bitch. I did not think this was particularly funny, but there was little else to be amused by. B could make even the blandest of jokes elicit a chuckle from his listeners. Perhaps the funniest thing of all was the way he laughed at his own jokes and stories. Personally, I thought it was a good thing the man was a teacher and not a performing comedian. He was a treasure and we loved and appreciated how he stuck by us, while most everyone else seemed to be avoiding us like the plague.

Towards the end of February 1952, Mama was ordered to appear at the police station. After some questioning she was handed a sheet of paper that apparently contained Papa's confession. "Your husband has willingly and without coercion supplied us with this confession, Mrs. Heinemann. Please read it over and sign it," the chief constable told her. Mama read the list of the many crimes Papa had supposedly committed against the Chinese people and thought she must have been given the confession of someone else. The man who allegedly perpetrated these crimes had about as much semblance to Papa as Papa did to Chairman Mao. She realized the whole thing was trumped up and contrived. If it was not for the seriousness of the situation, she would have found this ludicrous episode worthy of a good laugh. "I have been married to my husband for eighteen years and have never been aware of his leading a double life, I'm afraid. If indeed he is the horrible person that you have made him out to be, you should probably shoot him," Mama told the stunned official. "But as it stands, I have no knowledge of these activities and I don't recognize this man as my husband at all. He is about as capable of doing these things as a stuffed wolf is of devouring a lamb. I will not sign this under any circumstance." She pushed the bogus confession back into the hands of the constable and promptly left the station.

The authorities had hoped that she would sign the document so they could confront Papa with his wife's signature on his "confession." This ploy, I learned later, was designed to break a prisoner's spirit so he would admit his guilt. It apparently was a favourite technique of brain-washing, often employed by the authorities against prisoners whose confessions, true or not, formed an important part of their punishment and rehabilitation.

One of the first actions required of those arrested was the listing of the names of everyone with whom he or she had had contact, no matter how insignificant or seldom the contact. It seemed that Papa's name appeared on several such lists. When the number of people he met through his bookstore is considered, it was understandable how this practice led to his arrest. The authorities, quite ready and willing to go on the wildest of goose chases and the most inane of fishing expeditions, believed they had caught the kingpin of a spy ring. When I heard this, I was unable to suppress a giggle. The man simply did not posses the demeanour one would think was required to carry out such clandestine tasks. He could not speak, read, or write Chinese. These skills would be necessary, I thought, to be an effective gatherer of information, be it spy or otherwise.

Perhaps he had fooled us all, and Papa was a clever master of deceit and an agent in the employ of the British or Americans. This was unthinkable! Sure, Papa was gregarious, loved to tell stories, and was even prone to exaggerations. No doubt he had said things in conversations that were ill-conceived and politically incorrect, things that when taken out of context could easily be misconstrued. Papa was a clever man, no one could argue that, but in essence he was no more than a humble bookseller who loved people and saw only the good in them. Some would even have called him a bit naïve. I called him a sweet, trusting man. He would never hurt anyone or get involved in sinister plots. A case in point: Papa was coerced into compiling a list of his contacts for the authorities, which he did in abundance, but he only gave up names of those who had already left the country.

I had learned to admire Mama for her fearless pluck in the face of treacherous authorities and the uncertain future that hung over us. A number of times she was told she was free to take her children and leave the country. She steadfastly refused. "As long as my husband remains in custody I will wait here in Shanghai, even if it means living on the streets with my children. I will either bury him or leave the country with him. I will never abandon him, never!" she shouted into the face of a menacing looking official on more than one occasion. I was amazed by her chutzpah and, at the same time, was afraid she was pushing the wrong buttons and would get us all arrested. Luckily, Papa's persecutors seemed truly impressed by her courage and were maybe even a little intimidated by this diminutive Jewish woman. Whatever the case, she was never harassed by the authorities.

At one point in his incarceration, Papa felt in danger because he told his interrogators that a few American dollars had been secretly hidden in some books Mama had bound. Earlier during our stay in Shanghai, Mama, in order to complement Papa's love for books and to be able to serve the bookshop in some way, had learned the art of bookbinding from the wife of Lin Fu Ming, a French woman who was a master bookbinder. On occasion, some rare books needed to be rebound and Mama was thus able to do the task. With the onset of the Communist takeover, she had decided to use her craft to hide a few dollars for a time when the money would really be needed.

Days after Papa's confession, Mama faced the police, who had come to ransack our house in search of the illicit stash. They found the books and the money, and in triumph carried off the evidence. Mama expected to be arrested at any moment and for some time we lived with heightened apprehension. I continued my daily sausage selling rounds throughout these dramas, never knowing what I was going to find when I returned home. The anti-foreign rhetoric and propaganda, meanwhile, grew ever more strident, adding to our fears and concerns. The daily parades and loud patriotic music also continued to intrude. One could not escape the sonic attacks, especially from the roller rink across the street! Fortunately, Stephen was too young to grasp the situation. Mama and I attempted to lead our lives, depressing as they were, as normally as possible.

Shanghai, once one of the most notorious harbours in Asia, now boasted just a single drinking establishment near the waterfront. Only sailors who came off the few foreign merchant ships that docked nearby frequented it. In fact, the bar was there specifically for their convenience: the authorities did not want them wandering the streets of the city looking for entertainment and a place to drink.

The bar was owned and operated by a very large, unfriendly, one-eyed black American. Other than the few coloured U.S. military personnel I saw in town at the end of the war, he was the first African-American I got to know personally, albeit very peripherally. He was a man of few words and his imposing demeanour intimidated me. I never really learned his name. It was not a priority. To me he was just the owner of a bar where I delivered my wares to four beautiful White Russian girls he had in his employ. From the way he leered at me every time I visited the bar, I got the feeling he was sizing me up for future employment as one of his "girls." The Communist authorities tightly controlled the whole operation; every one of the girls was licensed and frequently checked out by the local cops to make sure their paperwork was up to date. Many of these young ladies of the night turned out to be my best customers. On a dreadfully cold, wet spring day, as we huddled by the coal stove-the only source of heat in the bar, the police arrived on their regular visit and immediately noticed the presence of a new face. The girls, who were fluent in Chinese, explained that I was there to deliver some sausages they had ordered. The contents of my suitcase and bags were closely examined, as was the permit I had been issued allowing me to conduct my delivery business. Some jokes were exchanged and the police departed, satisfied that I was not part of the entertainment. Still, it had been a trying experience for me. I was always worried I'd be hauled off like Papa on the least of pretexts. The girls, who considered themselves my unofficial protectors, could not hide that they were clearly nervous about my safety as well. After the police departed there was a distinct shift in mood from highly charged to almost relaxed. It was as if a predator had decided not to attack a nearby animal and wandered away because his belly was already full. This period of my life, although unhappy, was also the most interesting. I saw more of the city than ever before, met more people, and had more experiences than my adventurous soul could possibly have asked for.

Mama, in the meantime, continued her monthly visits to the horrible place where Papa was incarcerated. She had not laid eyes on him since the day of his arrest. Despite her ceaseless request to see him in person, she was never accommodated. I noticed that whenever Mama returned from a trip to the detention centre she was increasingly worried about his well-being. Still, she did not express her concerns to me. When I asked her about Papa, she was stoic and told me he would be fine, but her preoccupied demeanour told me otherwise. I never pursued the matter because I did not want to upset her. I left Mama to fret and brood in her own mind, just as I did in mine. Mama frequently made inquiries as to the progress of Papa's case and pressed the authorities for information about him. I believed her tenacity regarding Papa's welfare would sooner or later produce results. I only hoped those results would be his release, not a long sentence or, worse, his execution.

Whether grounded in paranoia or in fact, we felt we were being watched all the time and had given up using the phone because we knew it was tapped. Besides, very few people were still in touch with us. Everyone was nervous for their own safety and we had, for all intents and purposes, become persona non grata. The city seemed like a large depressed village. For the first time since my arrival in Shanghai I felt very ill at ease: I felt like a prisoner. I had never really thought I would want to leave, but I found myself thinking more and more about exactly that.

安娜樂麗

GOODBYE SHANGHAI

The spring of 1952 brought daily stories of suicides and arrests, as well as further incursions by the Chinese army into Tibet. Anti-foreign sentiment was growing, the great friendship between Russia and China was cooling off, and my family's situation remained unchanged.

On one particularly warm and sunny day, I was proceeding as usual to make a delivery. I walked slowly, unaware that a curtained police vehicle was following me. Although there was a curious crowd milling about and observing all this, none of it drew my attention. My mind was so preoccupied with Papa being kept in captivity and how his ordeal was affecting Mama and poor Stephen that I remained oblivious to everything around me. My little brother failed to understand why his father was not there for him and why Mama cried so much; he questioned me all the time about where Papa was. I truly did not know what to tell him for I lacked the answers he so desperately sought. How could I, a sixteen-year-old, explain to a four-year-old child that his father was falsely imprisoned? He questioned Mama and Amah but they did not know what to say to him, either. Amah, the dear soul she was, did her best to keep Stephen distracted and amused. She treated him like one of her own. Her devotion to our family was truly beyond the call of duty, not to mention brave considering we were a family whose head was accused of being a spy. These thoughts were sparking through my mind until I was suddenly snapped back into the moment, back into the harsh reality of the very unfriendly place that was Communist Shanghai. I was startled to find two soldiers, who had apparently disembarked from the vehicle shadowing me, holding my arms with vice-like grips. They firmly propelled me towards the curtained car, which had pulled slightly ahead of us to keep pace with our movement. It was all becoming very clear to me that this could be the beginning of the end for my family and me. I envisioned a joint operation in which Mama, too, was being rounded up at that very moment. Once I had been brusquely pushed into the back seat, we speedily left the slack-jawed crowd behind. I had drawn crowds before but never under such grim circumstances.

Thoughts rushed through my head like scudding storm clouds in a wintry sky. Nothing made sense. The Shanghai I had known for more than a decade had always been a city of intrigue and danger, but in a surreal sense. In all the years of Japanese occupation, the war, the misery of the ghetto, and the uncertainty of my future, I never felt threatened here. Shanghai had saved my life. Now I was beginning to wonder if it would be the city of my doom and that of my family.

We drove a short while in complete silence then entered through a gate and slammed to a stop in front of a four-storey brick building. My two guards led me inside and into a small room. The only furniture was an old uncluttered desk and two chairs. "Sit down," commanded one of the guards as he unceremoniously aimed me towards a chair. I did as he said and lowered myself into the chair directly in front of the desk. A moment later, a young man in the usual drab army uniform entered and dropped into the chair behind the desk. I looked at him with curiosity, wondering what I might be facing, and waited for him to confront me. He pretended not notice me and idly shuffled some papers on the desk. If this was a ploy to further unnerve me it had the desired effect. I dared not speak and did my utmost not to betray my fear.

After what seemed like an eternity, the officer looked up and fixed me with a long glance. He produced a pack of cigarettes and matches from one of his tunic pockets and fired up a smoke. I was somewhat surprised to notice that he had light-coloured eyes, which was unusual in Asians. I thought that perhaps one of his parents might have been a foreigner. When he finally addressed me in perfect English, my roving thoughts came to an abrupt end. "Miss Heinemann, how nice of you to join us. Would you care for a cigarette?" he said with forced politeness. I declined his offer. "I am going to ask you some questions, and you are going to answer truthfully, if you know what's good for you," he said, dropping me a half smile.

The first few questions were generic and pertained mostly to our everyday life and the Western Arts Gallery. These were not difficult to answer, but as he became more persistent in wanting information about Papa's business affairs, people he associated with, and activities I knew nothing about, I sensed a growing tension, sharpness of tone, and some impatience at my reluctance to answer. The officer abandoned his chair and moved to the edge of the desk, looking straight down into my eyes.

An adversarial note crept into the proceedings, as if he personally had something at stake to make this interrogation a successful one, and I was being of no help.

His increasing anger and impatience began to make me even more nervous and ill at ease. The officer launched himself from the desk and started to pace, stopping every so often, jabbing me with a finger to underscore remarks or questions. He butted out his half-smoked cigarette, snatched a pad and pencil from the desk and scribbled out a few Chinese characters. It was obvious that he was not used to dealing with young white females, especially one with an underlying attitude. His frustration manifested itself in a flushed face and tightening of the muscles in his neck which made the veins bulge out.

I became ever more silent, and he grew ever more insistent on getting the desired answers. Finally, in some anger and impatience of my own, I turned on him, much to his surprise. "I have no idea about Chinese parents and their children, sir, but European parents certainly are not in the habit of confiding their private affairs to their children. So, with all due respect, you can take it or leave it. I couldn't answer your questions even if I wanted to. I don't know anything!" I shouted, somewhat taken aback by my own boldness. There was a moment of deafening silence; he snapped the pencil he had been holding in two and flung the pieces at the wall. "You have not only proved to be uncooperative, you are being insolent to an officer of the People's Liberation Army. And you are certainly not showing me any due respect. I could have you shot, right now. Do you hear me? You are tempting fate. I have had people shot for less," he hammered back at me.

In exact opposition to the effect he hoped to have on me with this threat, I found myself becoming very calm, almost feeling a sense of relief that one way or another I was about to see this horror come to an end. "You go right ahead, sir, if you feel so inclined," I told him with a soft but firm voice. I could not believe what I had just said. I had really done it: I had just signed my own death warrant. The incensed officer twitched a crooked smile. I noticed his pale eyes had not only turned a shade darker since this interrogation began, but they were now awash with threatening overtones. He summoned the two guards who were waiting just outside the door. He barked some staccato-like orders at them and then turned to me. "Stand up!" he snapped. He cocked his head towards me; it was a signal for the guards to grab me. With the same vigour as when they had hoisted me from the sidewalk, they led me outside into a small courtyard and escorted me to a wall that was pockmarked from what was plainly the impact of countless bullets slamming into it. In conjunction with what can only be splatters of blood, the wall looked like some kind of abstract work of art.

My brain turned into porridge as the guards left me standing in front of the wall while they went back into the building. I waited for what seemed like hours but what in real time was probably only a minute or so. I watched four soldiers carrying rifles march into the courtyard. Not one sensible thought was able to penetrate my mind. Was this how my life would end, or was this a nightmare from which I would wake up at any moment? The soldiers lined up about fifteen feet in front of me and beheld me without interest. Why should they? They were professional soldiers for whom the taking of a life was nothing more than an order that they obeyed without question. After what seemed like another eternity, my interrogator strode into the courtyard like a man who was clearly on a mission. He walked right by the soldiers and approached me. "So, Missy, what do you think now? Is there anything you'd like to tell me?" he queried. I had resigned myself to my fate and without hesitation replied, "If this is the glorious Chinese revolution, I am not greatly impressed." He was angry and his hand flung out as if to strike me. I waited for it to sting my face, but the blow did not come. He snickered, gave me a look that seemed to be a contradictory mixture of contempt and admiration, then turned to the four soldiers and ordered them away. He gave me a curt bow and followed the soldiers into the building, leaving me standing in front of the wall. A few moments later the guards reappeared in the courtyard with my bags of sausages. They handed them to me, unlocked a heavy steel door in the wall, and pushed me through it. To my surprise I stumbled onto a side street. They brusquely waved me off and slammed the door shut. The nightmare was over!

It was still sunny and warm. The sky was blue–the bluest I had ever seen it. I heard some birds happily chirping, and I idly wondered how it was possible that life continued calmly all around me. People walked by going about their business, totally unaware of my ordeal and probably not caring much even if they had known. I stood on the side-walk and tried to pull myself together, but my knees were weak and felt as if they were going to buckle. I knew I could not remain standing there so I began to walk slowly, first in one direction, then another. I did not know where

I was and could not seem to organize my thoughts. As the events that had just transpired began to filter through my brain, the reality of how close I came to dying hit me hard. After a while of retracing my steps, I realized that I kept passing the building I was just in, and it occurred to me that this was not a good thing to be doing.

I decided to just walk in one direction, hoping eventually to find some familiar landmark that would help me find my way. After some time of aimless wandering, I found myself within a few blocks of home. It was getting dark and I was relieved to be in familiar surroundings. I was starting to feel like my old self again. One thing had become clear to me. I must absolutely not tell Mama of this episode because two things could happen: she might, in her anger, make some official complaint or, even worse, she might be reluctant to let me out of her sight again. Although I continued on my daily rounds after the unnerving incident with the firing squad, I did it with some apprehension that I might be picked up again.

The never-ending uncertainty of our future, the dwindling numbers of my customers, and the threat of the sausage factory closing made my daily life almost unbearable. I did my best not to show my unhappiness around the house or anywhere else for that matter; I knew I needed to be strong for my family.

The stress and constant worry Mama was enduring had turned her hair prematurely grey, and she spent more and more time crying. Dr. Blaschauer and I, meanwhile, had a falling out. One evening, when I came home much later than usual from my rounds, he tore into me that I should be thinking of Mama and not my own selfish pleasures.

"Don't you realize you are worrying her to death when you linger who knows where? You are old enough to know better," he said, concluding his little lecture. "Am I dismissed, Herr Professor?" was all I could think of saying, even though I had hardly lingered anywhere for my own selfish pleasures. It was obvious I had offended him, and it was the second to last conversation we would have. Perhaps I was out of line, but I was no longer a child and did not wish to be spoken to as one. Those were trying times for me as much as they were for Mama. I believed I was carrying more than my weight and helping out in every way possible. But I did not hold any animosity against Dr. B. I knew he loved Mama like a younger sister, perhaps even more deeply than that. I was convinced that if Papa had perished in captivity, he would have asked her to marry him.

One day flowed into another and the weeks disappeared into months. Life was like some senseless theatrical piece that had no audience and only Mama, Stephen, B, Amah, and me as its main characters. Another hot humid Shanghai summer had enveloped us and Mama had no energy. The only reasonably happy people were Stephen and his ever-cheerful caretaker, Amah. Although I was glad for Stephen and loved him dearly, I sometimes envied his innocence and inability to understand the drama of our lives. It seemed like only yesterday I had been in his situation with not a care in the world, while that world was falling apart in a terrible war that consigned fifty million people to their deaths. Even still, Stephen's childish antics often cheered me up after a weary day out on my sausage route. He had become quite fluent in Chinese and had learned to curse better than most pedicab drivers or coolies. It had become an embarrassment for Amah to take him out for walks, but the people in the neighbourhood loved the little golden-haired white boy who amused them with his colourful choice of words.

All around us we saw more and more evidence of the future Cultural Revolution. Teachers, intellectuals, and even professionals found themselves on farms helping with the harvest or being openly taunted and sometimes even physically abused. Not surprisingly, this behaviour was not only tolerated by the people in power but was also encouraged. The youth of the nation were becoming more militant and life for us got tougher every day. The number of students Dr. B taught became fewer, increasing the hardship of trying to make ends meet for everyone.

The first anniversary of Papa's arrest had come and gone without any kind of due process. No charges had been laid, no trial, no nothing. Or so we thought. Unbeknownst to us, he was taken to trial in December of 1952, after languishing in confinement for exactly one year. The trial was conducted entirely in Chinese, with no interpreter present. At the end of this sham, Papa was told that he had been sentenced to the time already spent in prison and that he would be subjected to immediate deportation. The second part of the sentence struck him as rather comical. China was the last place on earth he wanted to spend the remainder of his life: getting out as soon as possible was his only desire.

For us, meanwhile, Hanukkah and Christmas of 1952 were bleak, as we had no reason to celebrate. Stephen received some toys and woollen mitts that Mama had knitted for him. For me she knitted a beautiful woollen scarf to keep me warm on the cold winter walks delivering sausages. I gave Mama a pair of hand-embroidered slippers and a bottle of cheap perfume. She exhibited some signs of happiness and hugged me in gratitude, but the moment was short-lived. She was quickly overtaken again by melancholy and a sense of hopelessness, even guilt, that she had not been able to do anything for Papa. I reminded her that her loyalty, devotion, and refusal to leave him behind was the most noble and precious thing she could do for him. "Your love is keeping Papa alive, Mama. Don't ever forget that," I told her time and time again.

It was the 14th of January. I was out and about as usual taking care of business when Mama received the call she had waited an agonizing four hundred and five days to receive. It was a call from the detention centre to say that she could come and get her husband. She was stunned: "Should I bring a coffin?" is all she could utter. She was convinced she was being summoned to retrieve his corpse. "That will not be necessary, Mrs. Heinemann," the voice on the other end of the phone told her. "Your husband is being released from custody." No more was said. The caller hung up. She stood for a long moment staring into the receiver, the tone signal from the terminated call filling the air like some electronic insect. The reality of the situation finally hit her. Mama hung up and scurried downstairs into Dr. B's makeshift classroom. "B! B! Heinz is being released from prison. My husband is being set free! Come with me! We must go and fetch him at once!" she blurted out. B dismissed his handful of students and he and Mama set out for the detention centre.

The moment Mama had waited for so long had arrived, and she anxiously paced back and forth in one of the centre's offices while waiting to be reunited with Papa. Dr. B had decided to wait outside the building so Mama and Papa could have this special moment to themselves. When Papa finally entered the room, Mama could not believe she was looking at the man who had been part of her life for nearly twenty years. He was pale and had an extended belly from the beriberi. He was a mere shadow of his former self. His small figure was clad in a pair of pants held together by string, a worn shirt hung loosely on his thin shoulders, and a pair of ragged slippers barely stayed on his feet as he shuffled toward Mama. She knew that this was her dear husband. His grey eyes beamed the moment he saw her; a tired smile peaked through his lengthy beard. The Heinemann optimism and "never say die" attitude was there. He was quietly cheerful as they embraced. Mama was afraid to hug him too hard because he looked so fragile, but he clung to her as if he would never release her again. Other than having acquired the case of beriberi, which had resulted in the loss of all his teeth, he seemed well enough. He had lost something else, but this was something good to come out of the misery of the past year. The dust free, dry air of the jail, and not being able to smoke had resulted in the remission of his asthma. He was cured forever, even the resumption of smoking, a habit he dearly missed during confinement, did not trigger it. "Come, take me home my darling. I've had enough of this place," he finally said, reluctantly ending their embrace.

When they arrived back at Weihaiwei Road, Stephen was anxiously waiting the return of his father. At first he did not recognize the frail man with the lengthy hermit's beard. He clung shyly to Amah, who broke out in tears at the sight of her employer. "Come to Papa, Stephen. I've missed you," Papa said bending down to his knees and opening his arms. Amah gently nudged Stephen towards his father and they embraced. "You forgot to shave Papa," Stephen said, eliciting a chuckle from everyone. When I got home that night, I was totally surprised and overjoyed to see him. At first I noticed very little change in him except for the loss of weight and no teeth. He was dressed in his favourite pyjamas and dressing gown, seated in a comfortable chair, and savouring a cigarette. Fortunately for me, Mama had spruced him up to look more like his old self so I did not have to go through the shock of seeing him as he first appeared upon his release. He had bathed and shorn off the beard. Still, I started noticing the changes in him quickly enough.

After the first exchange of joyful greetings, he lapsed into silence or only spoke in a barely audible voice. Over the next few days he related his time in prison, haltingly, and in whispers. The full account of his time spent in hell would take many years to be revealed, told in fragments: sometimes the information would be repetitive, at other times new revelations were added. We finally started to understand the full extent of his ordeal and the details of why he had been arrested. While in prison, the authorities had attempted to prove that Papa was a spy for the Americans and that he had sent coded information in books and newspapers out of the country. They must have realized, however, that he did not have the personality, nor the proficiency in the language to be a spy. Most shocking of all was that they were able to repeat conversations he and Mama had in the privacy of their bedroom, hence his reluctance to speak and then only in whispers.

Papa seemed subdued, nervous, and worried that his plight might not be over. He was right: it was not quite over. Until we were able to depart by train for Canton, scheduled by the authorities for January 21, 1953, he had been ordered to go to the local police station each day and give an account of his daily activities. One of the first requests Papa made of me upon his return was that I immediately leave my job. During captivity he had been told of my daily toils selling sausages on the streets of Shanghai. It had distressed this proud man that his sixteen-year-old daughter worked because he was unable to provide for his family. I could not refuse his request, though it was with mixed feelings that I acquiesced. I was giving up certain independence and it reminded me that I was not yet an adult who could choose her own way in life.

It now became a daily game to figure out what else could go wrong with our lives, but it seemed that our dark cloud had lifted. Papa slipped into a daily routine of visiting the police station without further incident and I, being jobless, helped out as much as I could around the house. Once again plans were put into place for our departure to Canada. Because the original emigration paperwork had been processed during the summer and fall of 1950, some of the documents such as our Provisional Certificate of Nationality, which was required to enter Canada and the countries en route, had to be reissued. Most of the belongings we crated a year earlier were still sealed with the official export papers intact, so all we needed to do was pack our suitcases. Although we were of the belief that nothing would come in the way of our leaving Shanghai this time, an underlying tension kept us all in its grip.

Nº 31277

EE/75 (Revised)

PROVISIONAL CERTIFICATE OF NATIONALITY
CERTIFICAT PROVISOIRE DE NATIONALITÉ
VORLÄUFIGE NATIONALITÄTS-BESCHEINIGUNG

This is to certify that HEINEMANN Paula-K. states that (she) is a German national by virtue of* birth and that there is no reason to doubt (her) statement.

This Certificate is valid only for the journey to the Western Zones of Germany, within 6 months from the date thereof, and must be surrendered to the Burgomaster in the place of destination immediately after issue of ration card, identity card, and residence permit.

It does not exempt the holder from compliance with any travel regulations in force in Germany or elsewhere or from obtaining a visa where necessary.

Il est certifié par le présent document que HEINEMANN Paula-K. déclare qu'elle est de nationalité allemande par* naissance et qu'il n'y a pas de raison de mettre en doute sa déclaration.

Ce certificat n'est valable que pour un voyage à destination des Zones Occidentales d'Allemagne, pour une durée de 6 mois à partir de la date de délivrance, et doit être remis aux Maire du lieu de destination immédiatement après délivrance de la carte de rationnement, de la carte d'identité, et du permis de séjour.

Il n'exempte pas le titulaire des règles de circulation en vigueur en Allemagne ou ailleurs ni de l'obtenation de visas nécessaires.

Hiermit wird bestätigt, daß HEINEMANN Paula-Kaete *erklärt, daß (sie) durch** geburt *deutscher Staatsangehöriger ist und daß kein Grund vorliegt, (ihre) Angaben zu bezweifeln.*

Diese Bescheinigung ist nur gültig für die Reise in die Westzonen von Deutschland, innerhalb von 6 Monaten vom Ausstellungsdatum ab, und muß sofort nach Ausstellung der Lebensmittelkarte, Kennkarte und Aufenthaltsbewilligung dem Bürgermeister im Bestimmungsort abgegeben werden.

Es befreit den Inhaber nicht von den in Deutschland oder anderswo gültigen Reisevorschriften oder, wenn erforderlich, von der Erlangung eines Sichtvermerks.

Description
Signalement
Beschreibung

Profession / Profession / *Beruf*	Dentist
Place and Date of Birth / Lieu et date de naissance / *Geburtsort und -datum*	BERLIN, 21-7-1910
Height / Taille / *Größe*	1 m 60
Colour of Eyes / Couleur des yeux / *Augenfarbe*	grey
Colour of Hair / Cheveux / *Haarfarbe*	dark blond
Signature of Bearer / Signature du Titulaire / *Unterschrift des Inhabers*	none

Accompanied by the following minor children:
Accompagné par les enfants mineurs suivants:
Begleitet von den folgenden minderjährigen Kindern:

	Name / Nom / *Name*	Date of Birth / Date de naissance / *Geburtsdatum*	Sex / Sexe / *Geschlecht*
(i)	HEINEMANN Hannelore	29 février 1936	female
(ii)	HEINEMANN Stephen Richard	11 mars 1947	male

AFFAIRES ÉTRANGÈRES 500 FRANCS
AFFAIRES ÉTRANGÈRES 1000 FRANCS
22 AOUT 50

Pour le Consul Général
L'ATTACHÉ DE CONSULAT

Signed / Signé / *Unterschrift*: C. Ledan
C. LEDAN

Date / Le / *Datum*: Changhai, le 22 Août 1950./.

"naturalisation" or "marriage".

See over for visas.

Provisional Certificate of Nationality, August 22, 1950

UNITED NATIONS
RELIEF AND REHABILITATION ADMINISTRATION
CHINA OFFICE
235 Nanking Road
Shanghai

IN REPLY REFER TO:

May 2, 1947

TO WHOM IT MAY CONCERN

This is to certify that HEINEMANN, Heinz-Egon, Paula, Hannelore & Stefen R. are bona-fide Displaced Persons of German nationality. They are registered with this Office and are eligible for U.N.R.R.A. assistance.

Thomas Pym Cope
Director,
Repatriation Branch Office,
Displaced Persons Division.

U.N.R.R.A.
MAY 2 1947
SHANGHAI

United Nations Displaced Persons letter, May 2, 1947

On one of the last days Papa had to appear at the police station, he failed to arrive home when expected. Mama paced nervously, trying not to panic and imagine the worst case scenario. Just as she was about to break down, she received a call informing her that there had been an accident and that Papa was in the hospital with a crushed left elbow. Not much explanation was given other than that the pedicab Papa was in had been in a collision with a bus. Although horrified, it came as a relief to Mama and me that he had not been arrested again. She was assured that well-trained orthopaedic surgeons were tending to Papa and that the elbow and arm would be saved and heal properly.

Although Papa did receive the finest of care, the injury would serve as a reminder of that day for the rest of his life. He would regain only limited use of the arm, never being able to raise it above shoulder height. According to details later given by Papa, a city emergency vehicle had pulled away from the curb into traffic, apparently without noticing the pedicab. In order to avoid the vehicle, the pedicab driver made an evasive manoeuvre. It resulted in the collision with the bus that had also just pulled into traffic behind them after making a scheduled stop. The pedicab was almost totally demolished in the crash. Miraculously, Papa and the driver survived but not without injury.

The nature of the accident convinced Papa, who without question had acquired a severe case of paranoia, that there was a conspiracy against him by the Communists to eliminate him before he could leave the country. "I'm telling you this was no accident. The driver of the emergency vehicle deliberately pulled out in front of us," he told us after we got him home from the hospital. "We won't be safe until we are out of Shanghai...if we get out." It was one of the few times I heard him talk like that: deserted by his usual optimism and afraid for our lives.

Mama, however, kept her head and, being the resourceful person she was, looked for a new angle to turn this latest misfortune into our favour. She spent the next few days trying to convince the authorities that with Papa's frail health and the additional injury that had his left arm in a massive cast, the family should leave Shanghai by ship and not be subjected to an arduous train journey. In what seemed to be the first act of compassion by a regime that had caused us so much sorrow over the past few years, or because they were tired of dealing with this relentless woman, they granted permission for us to leave by sea. We were all relieved to not have to endure the harrowing three-day train voyage to Canton, with its attendant dangers and discomforts. Our new departure date was set for March 23, 1953. It was the day of Papa's forty-first birthday and, for him, it was the best gift he could have received. Although he was in quite a bit of pain, his spirit started lifting and we made our final preparations to leave.

With just a few days left before leaving Shanghai we said our goodbyes, the most difficult of which was parting with Amah. It was especially hard on Stephen, and tears flowed on this sad occasion. It had been decided that Dr. B, who had continued to use the old bookshop as a classroom, would move into the Weihaiwei premises. Mama and Papa had created a comfortable home there with quite a number of fine pieces of furniture. They did not want to abandon their belongings to the Communists. It was the second time in their lives that they were to walk away from everything and into the unknown. This time, they left behind not only possessions accumulated over the many years in Shanghai, but unrealised dreams. Greater still, we left behind my beloved grandfather who laid buried in Chinese soil. Though we were optimistic and looking forward to a new life in freedom, we all had feelings of sadness.

On the morning of March 22, one day before our official departure, a hired vehicle came to take us to the waiting ship in the harbour of Hongkew, not far from the pier we had arrived at almost fourteen years earlier on the *Julio César*. When we were ready to leave, the good Dr. B approached me with a small sardonic smile pasted on his face. I was not sure what to make of it. "I know we have had our differences but we should not part as enemies," he said, much to my surprise. "Not that I believe we ever were enemies, just not on speaking terms, I guess you could say. So that being said, I wish you the best of luck, Hannelore. I will never forget you. I hope you will think of me once in a while." I assured him I would never forget him and thanked him for all his support. I was actually quite moved by this overture of peace. He shook my hand and came near to giving me a hug from which we both shied away. It was an awkward moment, but I was happy to leave knowing he had put aside his anger and that we were parting without rancour.

Some time later we boarded the ship. Unlike the luxurious vessel that had brought us to Shanghai, our ship of departure was a nondescript freighter belonging to the British fleet of Jardine Matheson. We were the only passengers. To the very last moment, the Chinese authorities remained in character and played out their ludicrous charade. Papa was under a form of house arrest. Two guards were stationed at our cabin door to make sure he remained there until the ship had left the harbour. It seemed that as long as Papa was in Chinese territory he was considered an enemy of the state. We spent our last night in China quietly anticipating our departure and wondering if anything else could possibly go wrong. We should have been elated but we were all very tense. The guards at our cabin door only intensified our insecurities. Was this all too good to be true, or were we finally going to get on with our lives?

After a restless night, Stephen and I rose early and wandered out on deck. It was the morning of our much anticipated departure. A pale wintry sun glinted on the calm waters of the Whangpoo River, giving it a burnished appearance. A few sampans were listlessly bobbing nearby. We had not been on deck long when the usual blast of the ship's horn was sounded to announce that the voyage was about to begin. Moments later, the crew was busy getting us underway. The lines were slipped from the moorings; the ship was released from the constraints that held it to Communist soil. It struck me as a fitting metaphor for our journey into freedom. Soon a deep throbbing vibration, with an accompanying shudder, announced that the voyage was about to begin. The vessel stirred into motion and, at a snail's pace, manoeuvred into the middle of the river. I watched with nervous excitement as we knifed into the ever-widening waters of the Yangtze River Delta. The famous Shanghai skyline faded into the distance as we picked up speed. It was a bittersweet moment. Stephen and I watched silently as we approached open waters and felt the roll of the ship increase. "Do you think we'll ever come back, Hannah?" he asked. "I don't know, Stephen. Perhaps some day when we live in a saner world," was my reply, wondering if such a day would ever come.

A rapidly approaching launch suddenly caught my eye and I noticed that our ship had cut its speed. My heart started pounding as a rope ladder was lowered along the side of the ship as the launch drew near. Then, I saw the two guards who had been stationed at our cabin door walk to the railing. With an enormous sigh of relief I watched the men clamber over the railing and down the ladder to the launch. As soon as they stepped onto the launch it sped off into the mist towards Shanghai, a city in which we had spent fourteen years of our lives. They had been fourteen years of challenge laced with joys and sadness.

I took one long final glance in the direction of the city that had been my home throughout most of my childhood. The city saved my life and that of Mama, Papa, and Opa. It had been a haven for thousands of fellow Jews during one of the worst periods in human history. I knew that Shanghai would always occupy a corner of my heart.

Stephen and I went below and joined Mama and Papa in our cabin and together we savoured the knowledge of having reached international waters. There was a discreet knock on the cabin door. For a moment we tensed up, but we were quickly put at ease by a smiling captain with outstretched hand. "Congratulations, Mr. and Mrs. Heinemann," he said. "You and your family are now free."